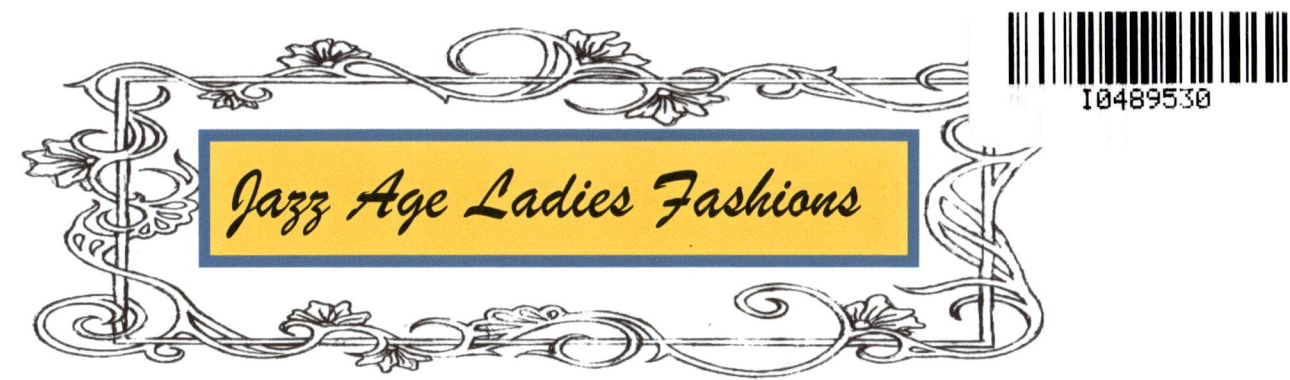

Jazz Age Ladies Fashions

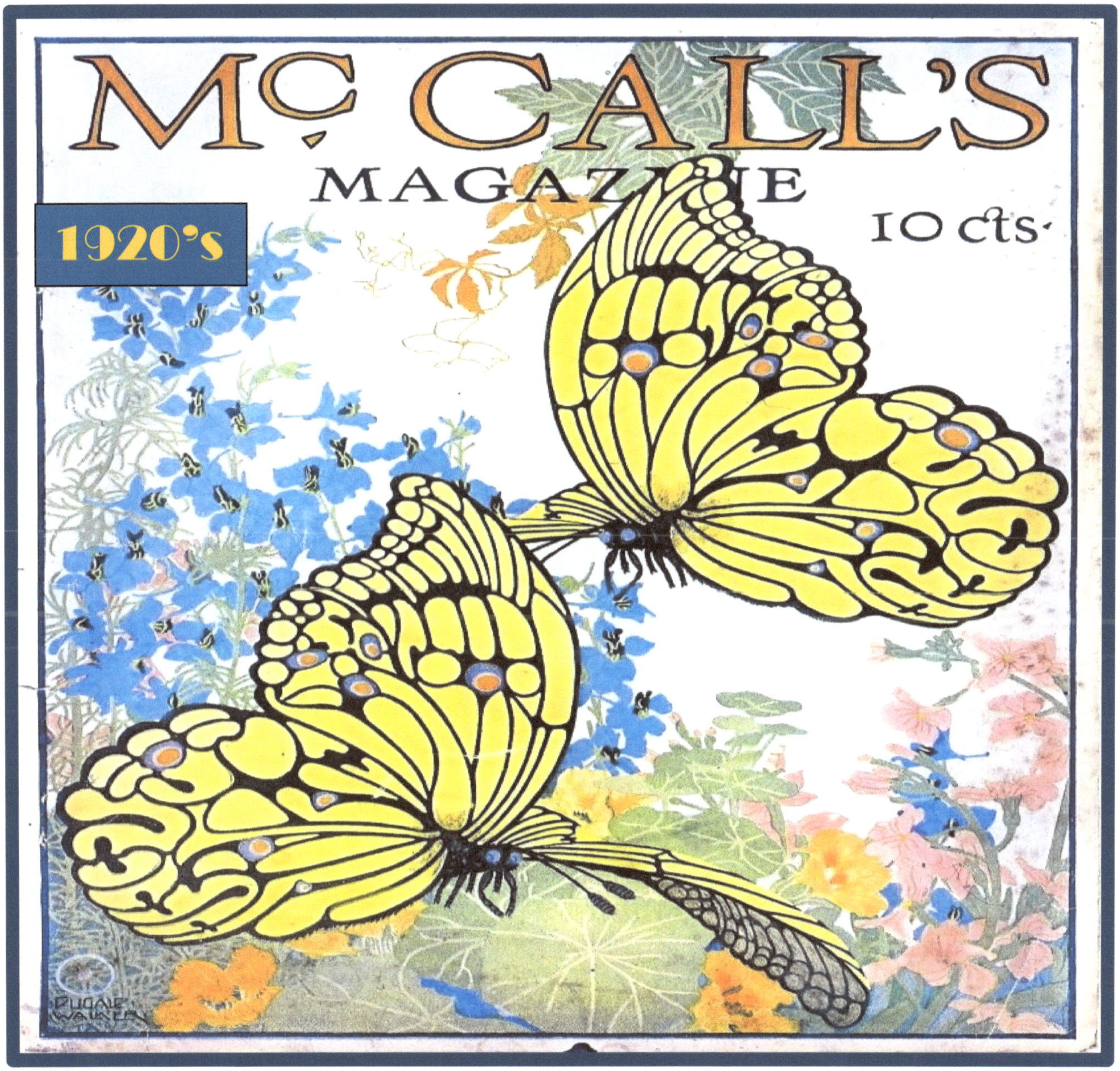

1920's

McCALL'S MAGAZINE

10 cts.

Cynthia Gallant-Simpson

Coloring Book for Grownups

Published by ~

Hesperus ART & INK

Blue Hill, Maine 04614

Author's Inspiration

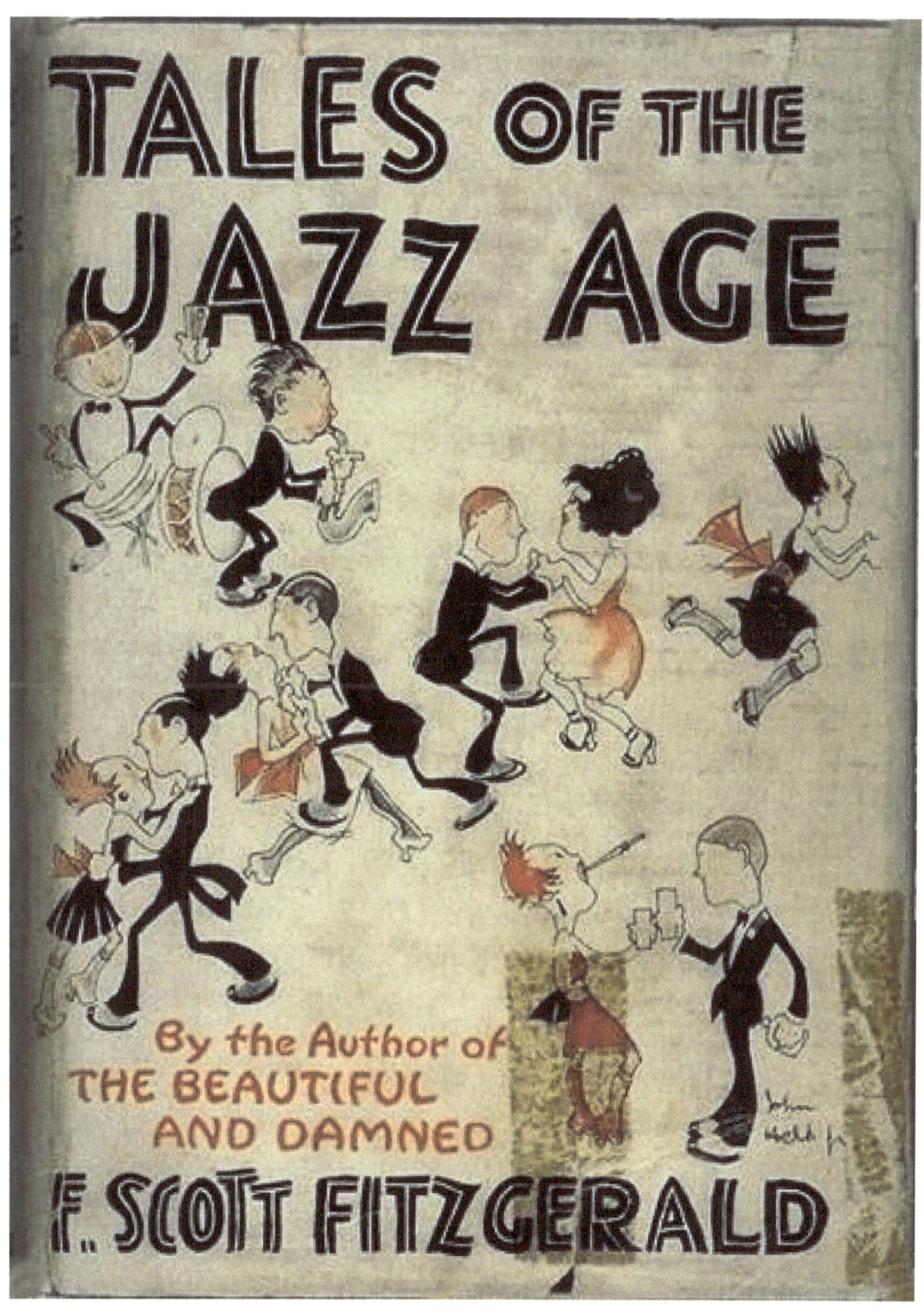

TALES OF THE JAZZ AGE

By the Author of
THE BEAUTIFUL
AND DAMNED

F. SCOTT FITZGERALD

Hello,

My favorite activity as a child, other than reading, was coloring. I particularly loved the movie star coloring books that let me be the costume designer...at least to decide on the colors.

I have always loved fashion, and even did some professional modeling to help defray college tuition. I think in outfits, whether I am going out to rake leaves, head to the grocery store, or prepare for a night on the town.

I would neither think of wearing a mix of gold and silver jewelry nor fail to choose the right shoes to compliment my outfit.

Most of all, I love color. As a painter of Americana Folk/Primtive Art, color rules my life and my work. I find joy in what happens when colors meet and play off one another. Colors are palpable for me. In my twenties, when I discovered F. Scott Fitzgerald's books, I fell in love with the period of the twenties, and the great women's fashions of the tumultous jazz years.

I work principaly in acrylics and you could paint in this coloring book by putting a piece of cardboard or other protection under the page you are working on however, I recommend well sharpened colored pencils or, of course, crayons. However, crayons may not allow you to work with the fine details.

However you choose to enjoy this book of flapper fashions, I wish you the best and hope you will recommend it to friends.

Cynthia

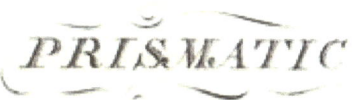

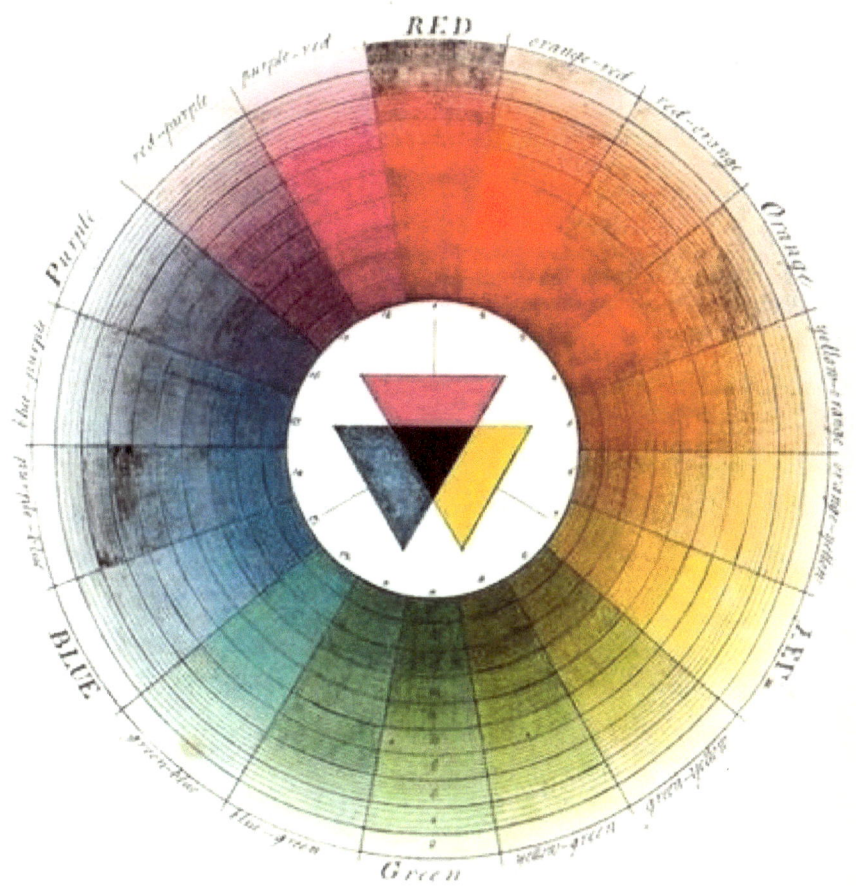

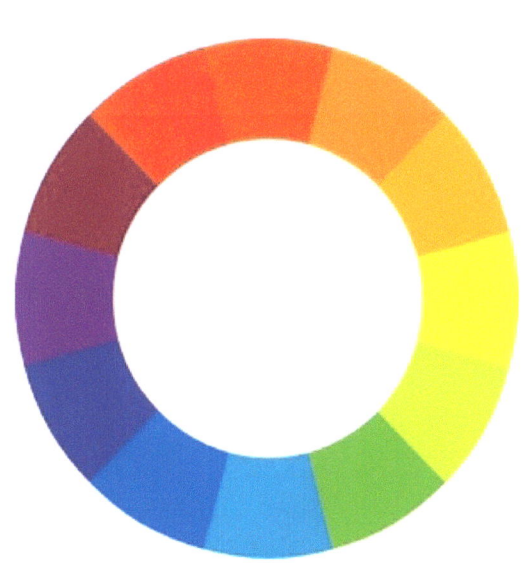

The art movements of the Twenties were Surrealism and Art Deco. However, it was Art Deco that had the strongest influence on the period's women's fashions and home decorating. We would remiss by not including those women whose ideas and actions set the ball rolling for the women of the twenties...the women who, early in the new century, took the first brave and vital steps toward women's rights.

Illustrator Charles Dana Gibson considered his creation of the girl who came to be known as the "Gibson Girl" to be a composite that represented "thousands of American girls." Girls and women were already flirting with independence and laying the groundwork for the next generation who would follow in their footsteps... but take far larger steps and make a more longlasting impact on the American scene for all women. First they let down their hair, and then they bobbed it off. They threw off corsets and crinolines in favor of loosely draped clothes and proceeded to dance, drink and swear. Let's hear it for those brazen flappers!

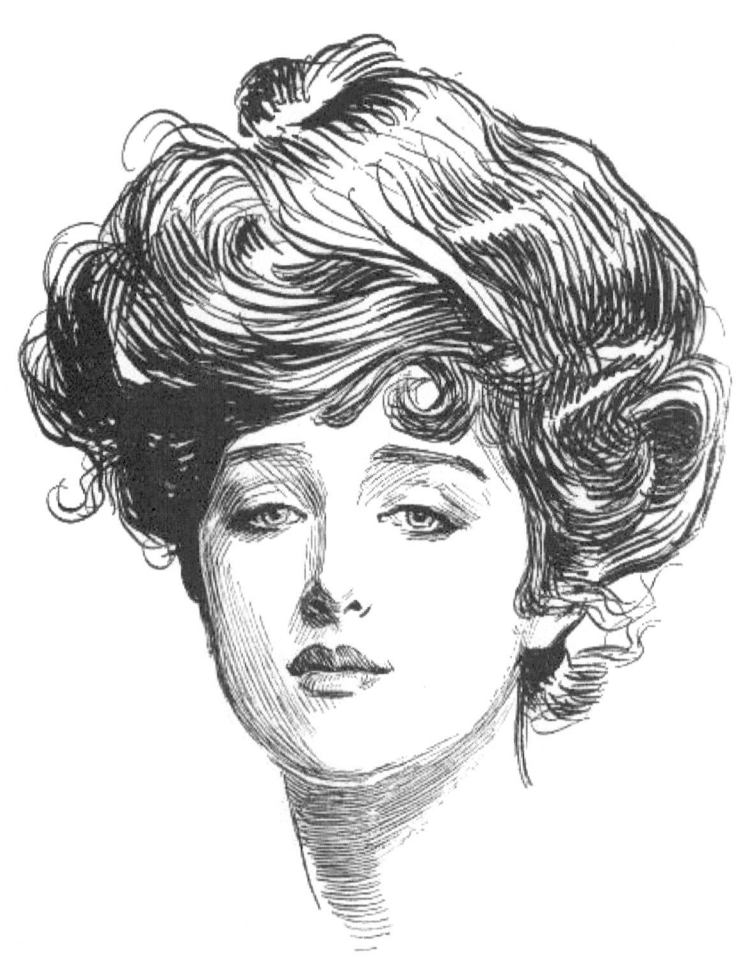

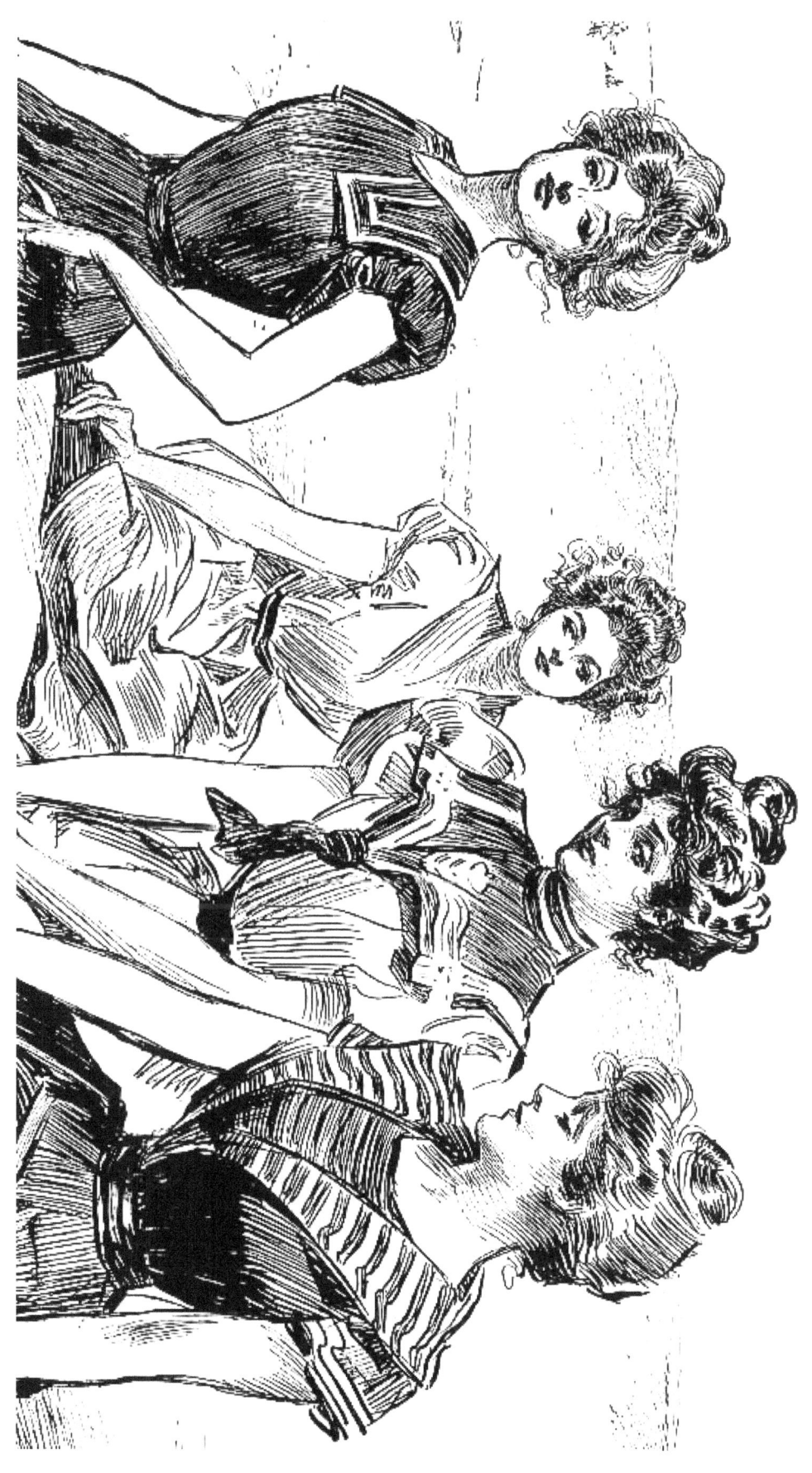

A variation on the Gibson Girl

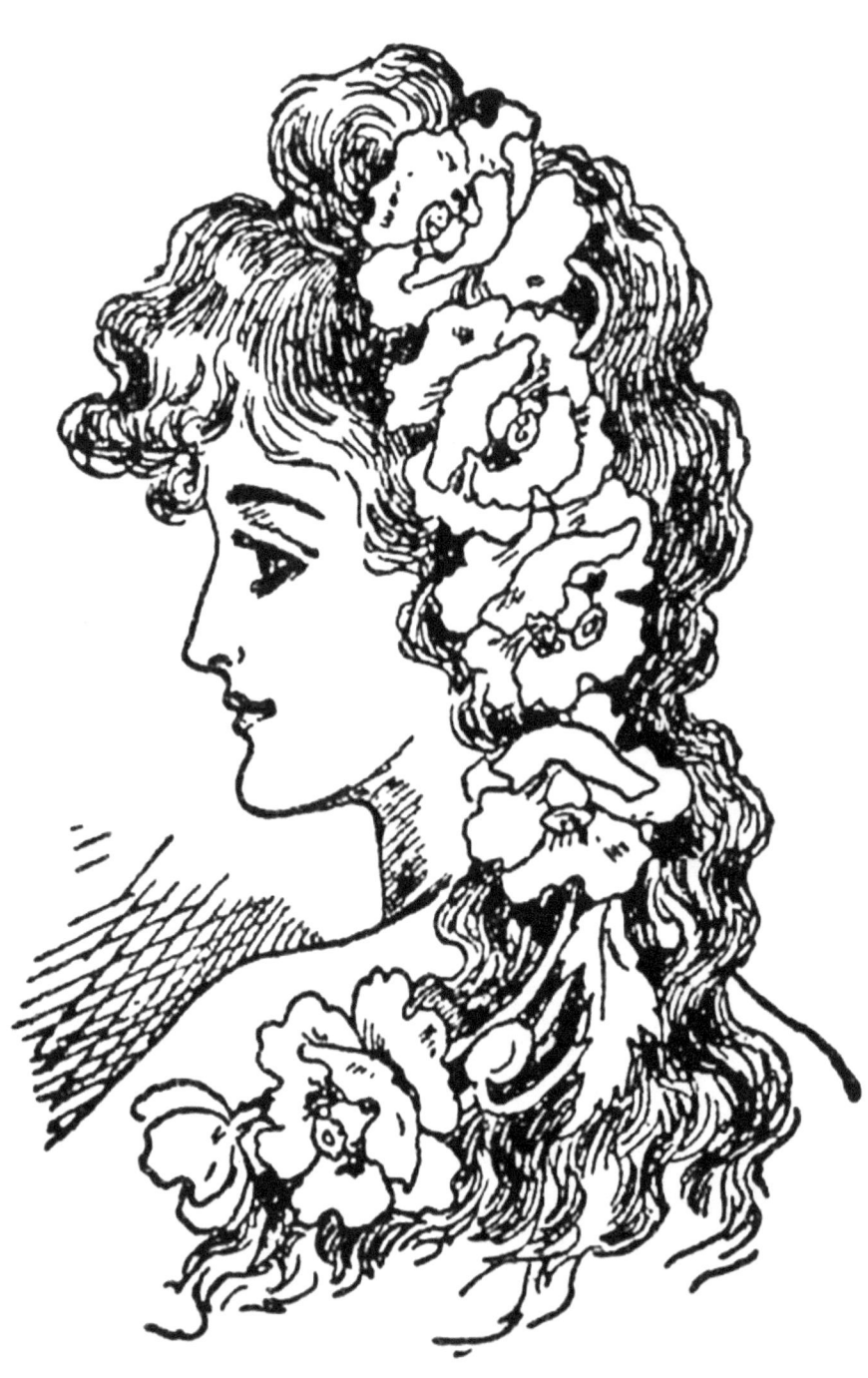

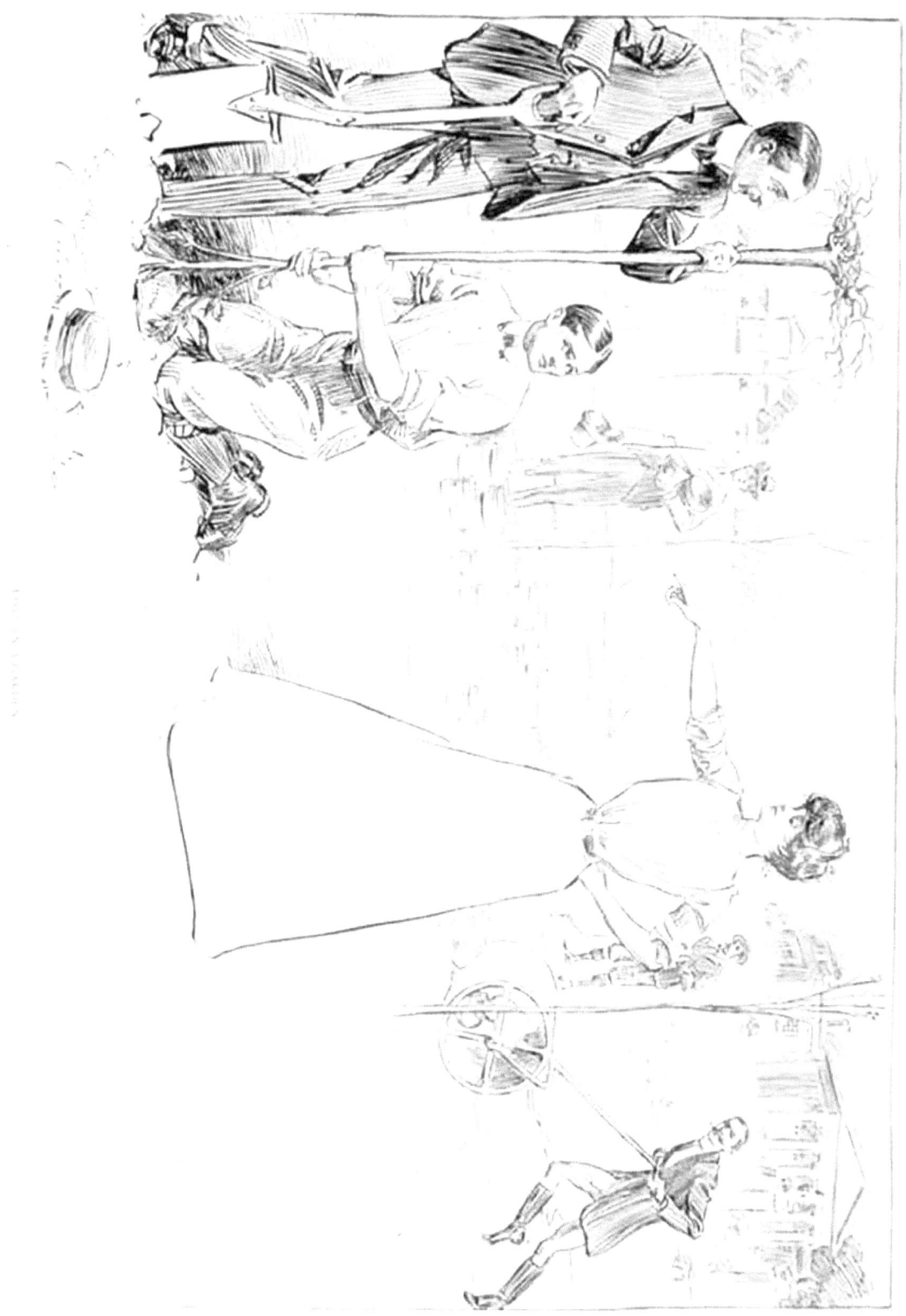

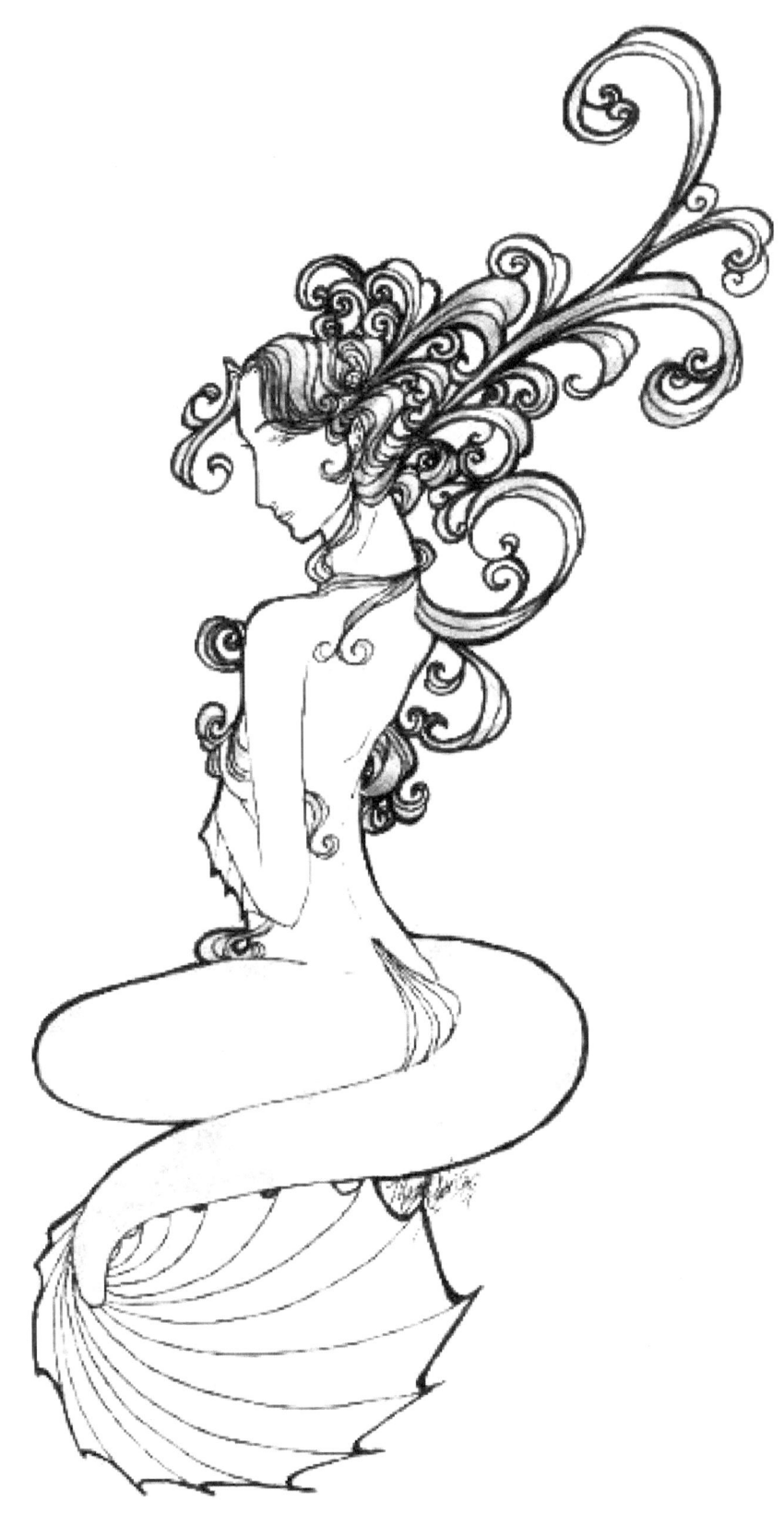

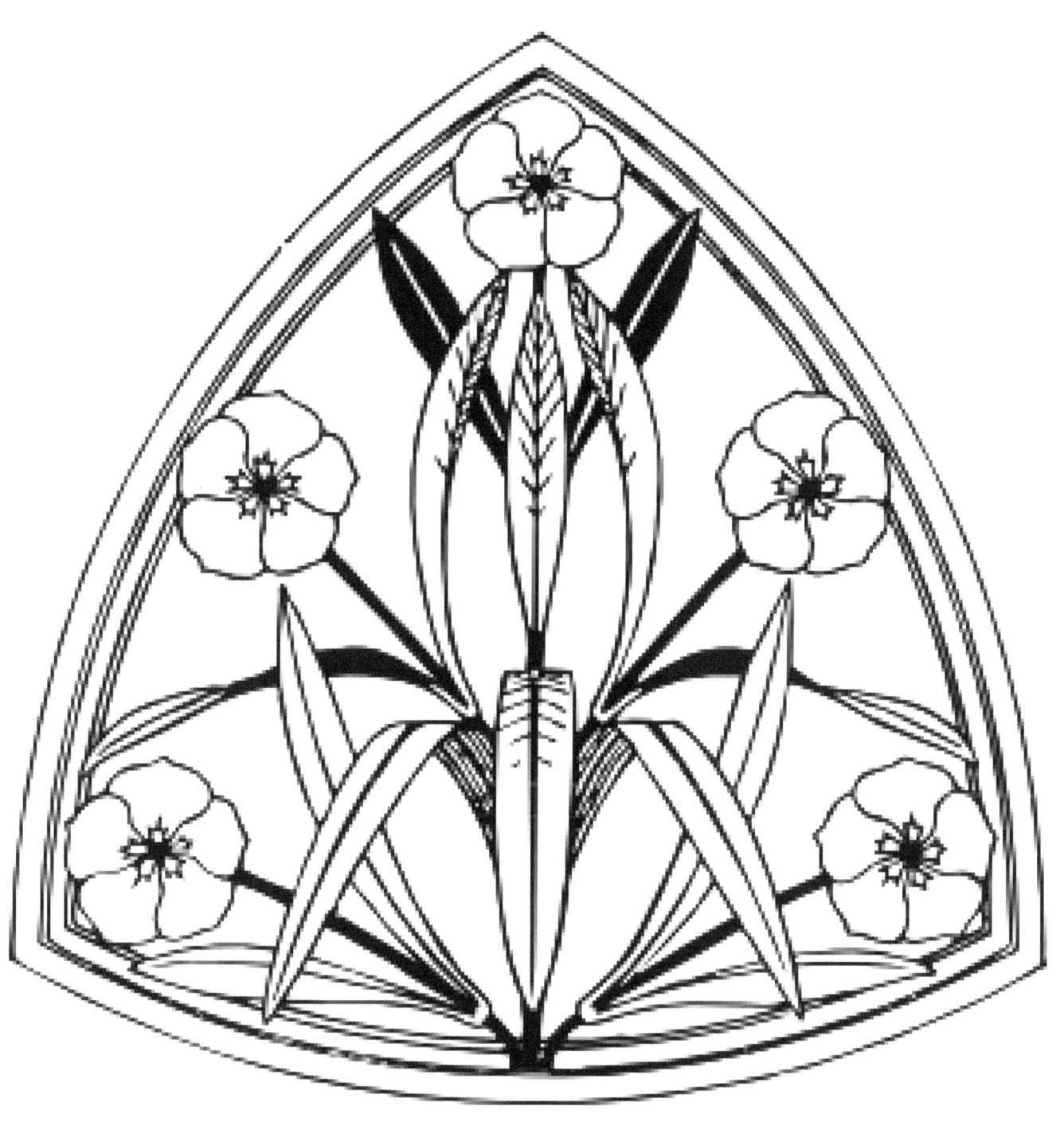

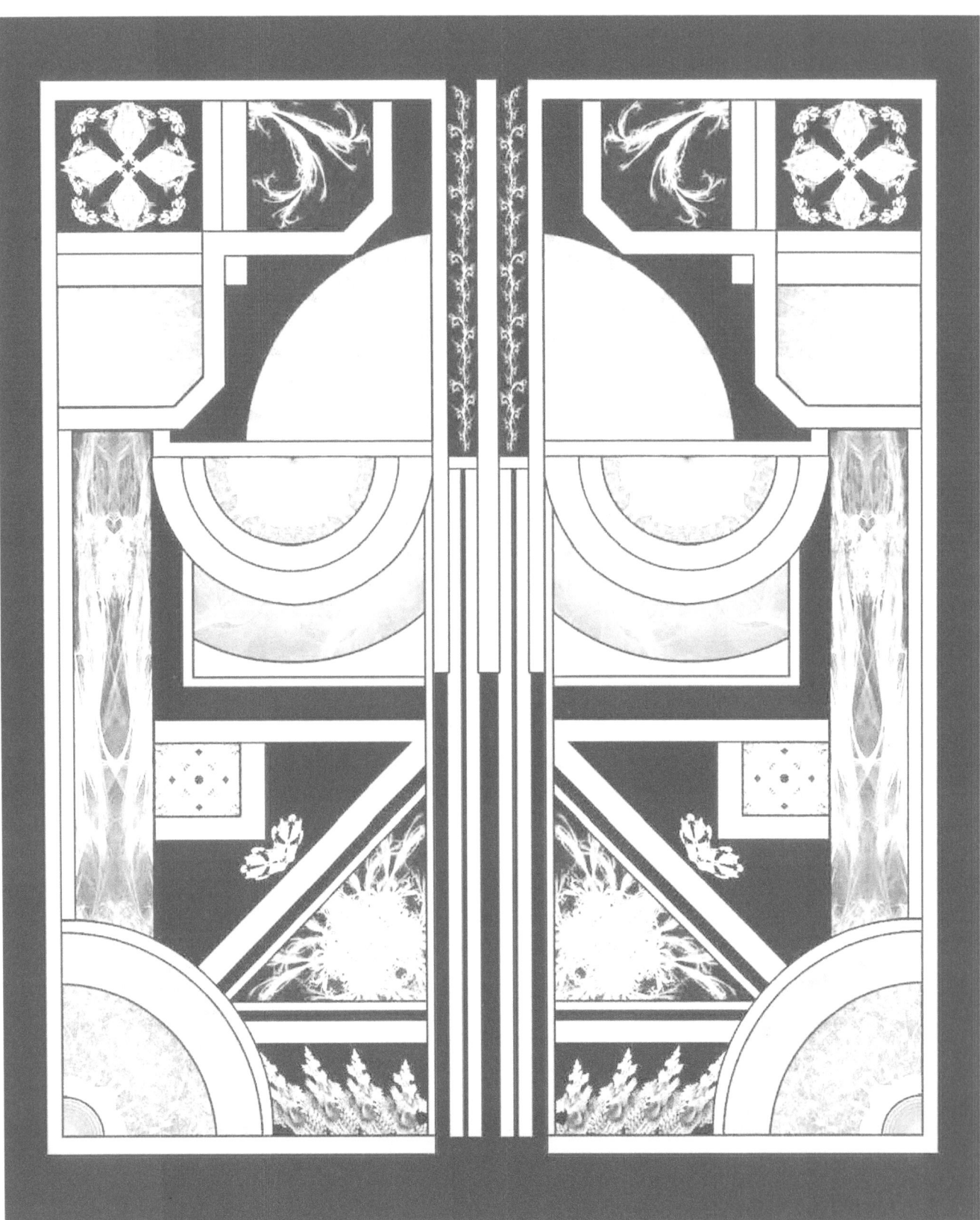

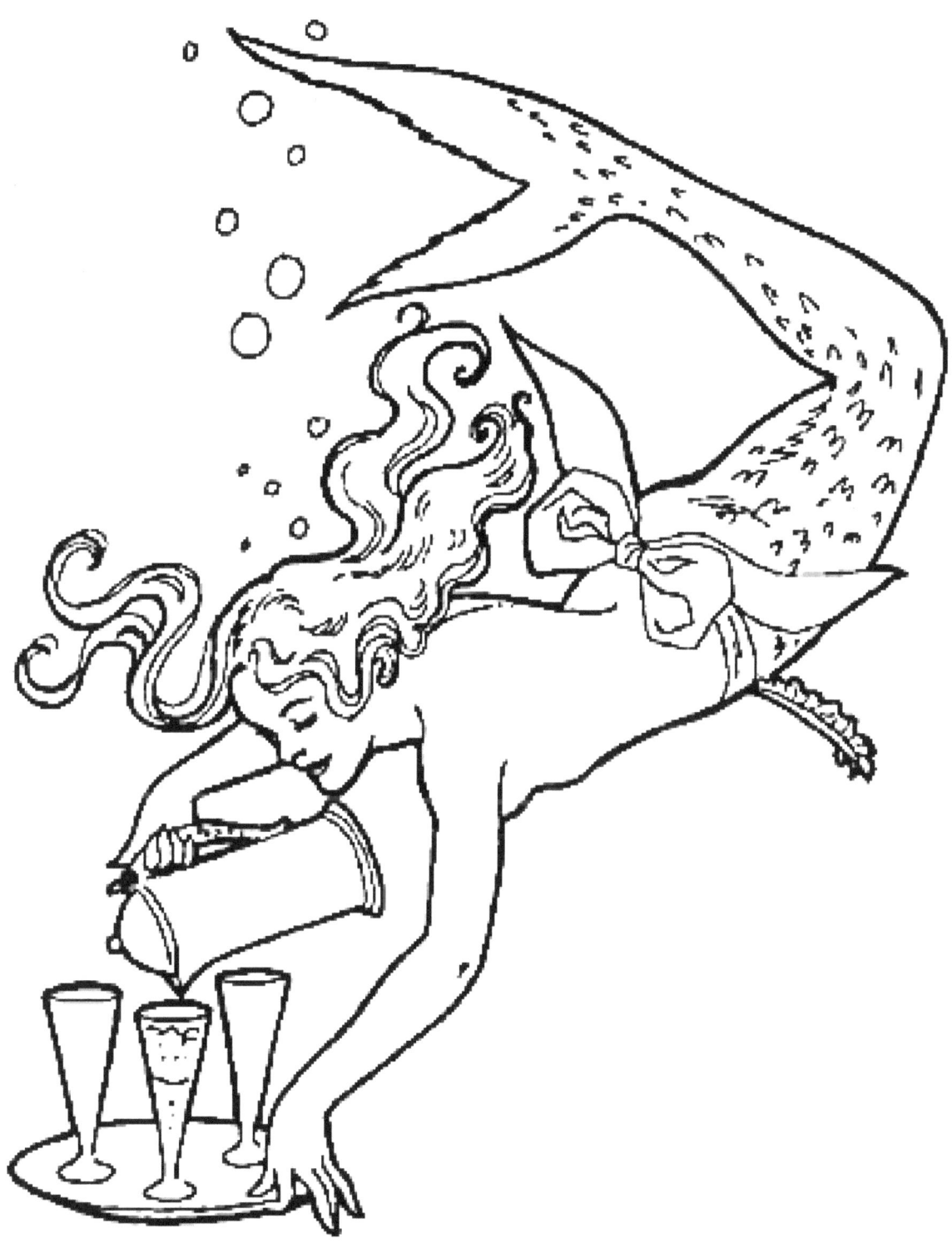

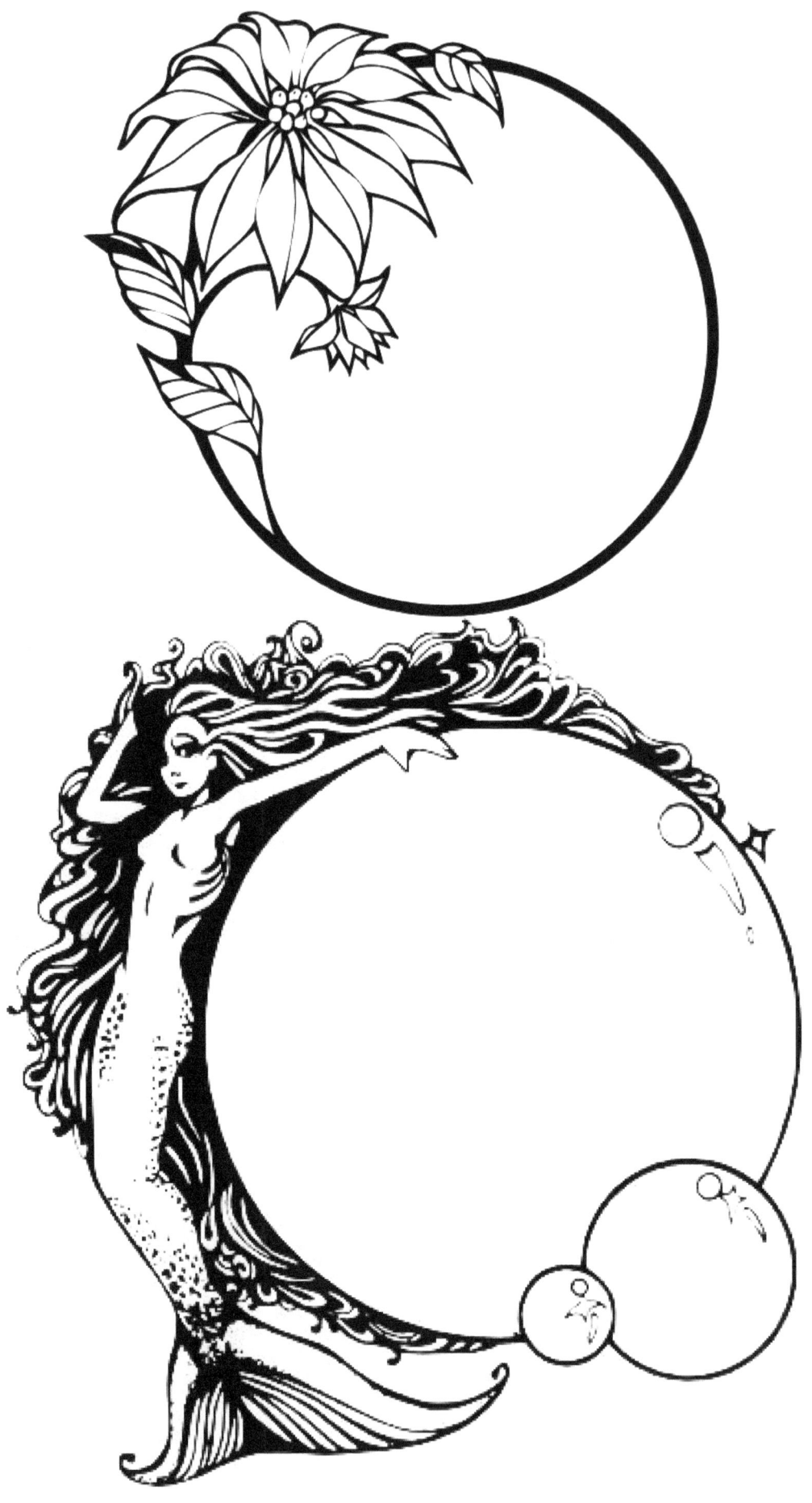

Welcome to the Roaring Twenties!

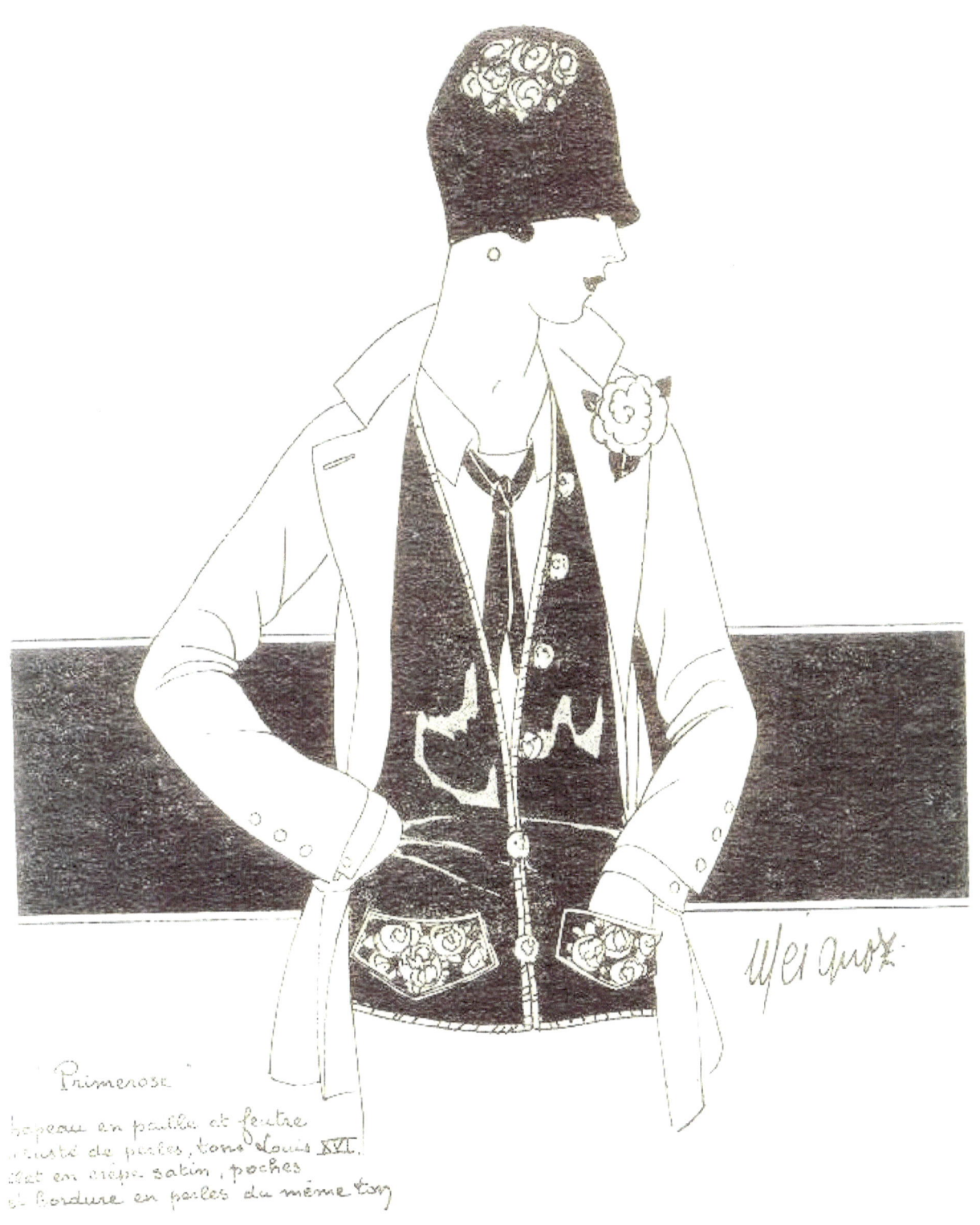

Note: Art Deco influence on pockets and hat.

The all-essential flapper hat

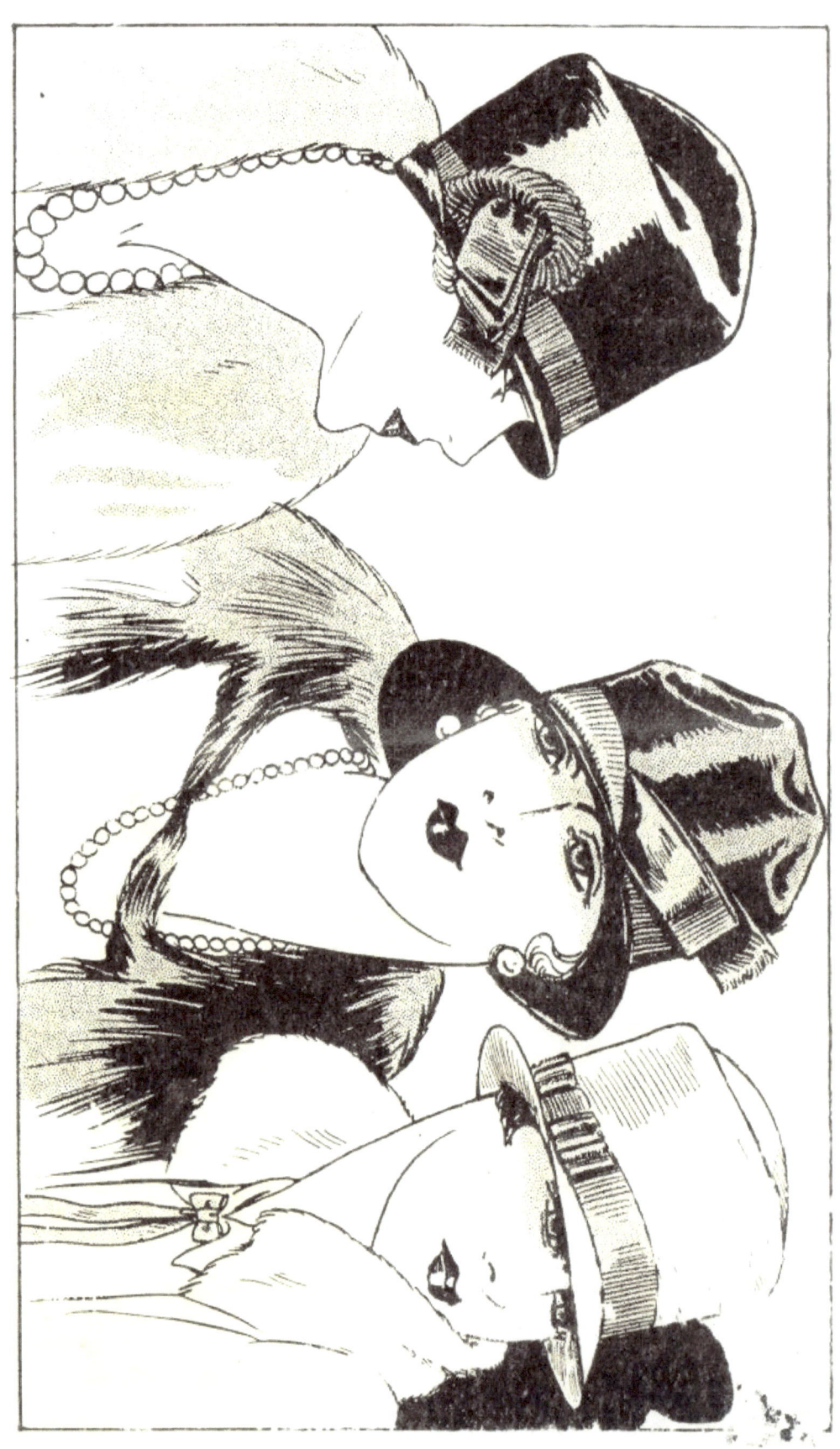

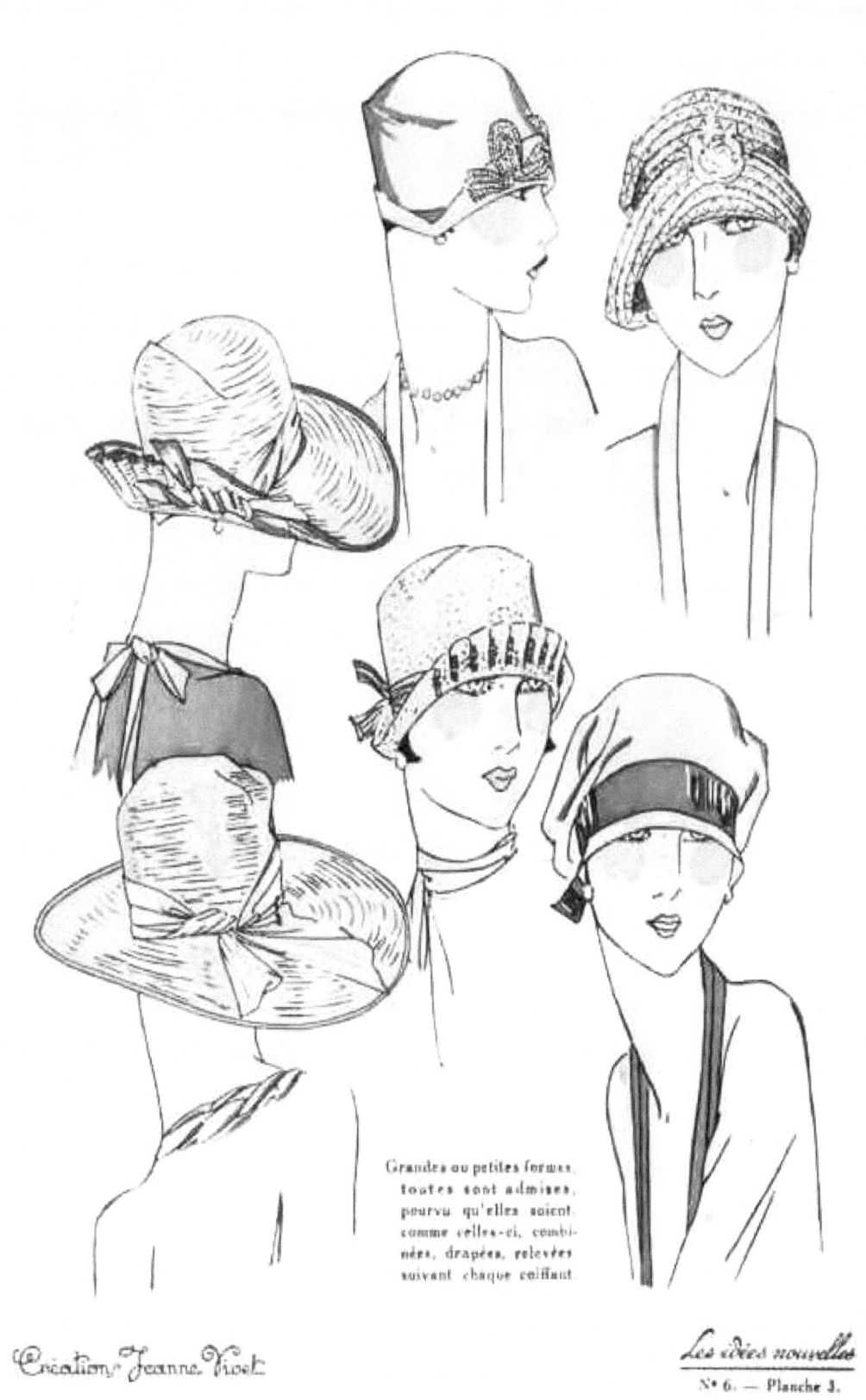

Grandes ou petites formes,
toutes sont admises,
pourvu qu'elles soient
comme celles-ci, combi-
nées, drapées, relevées
suivant chaque coiffant.

Créations Jeanne Viot

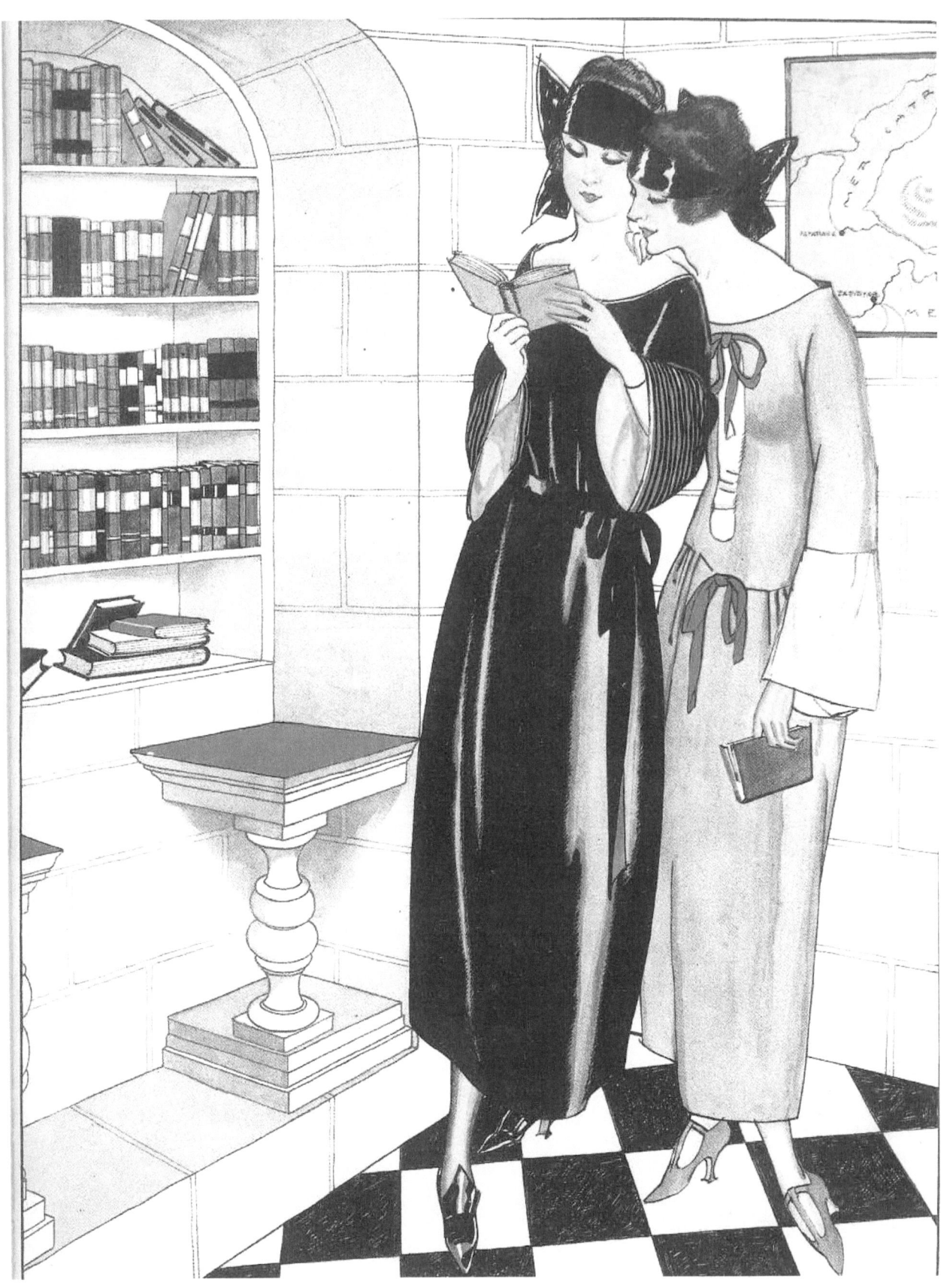

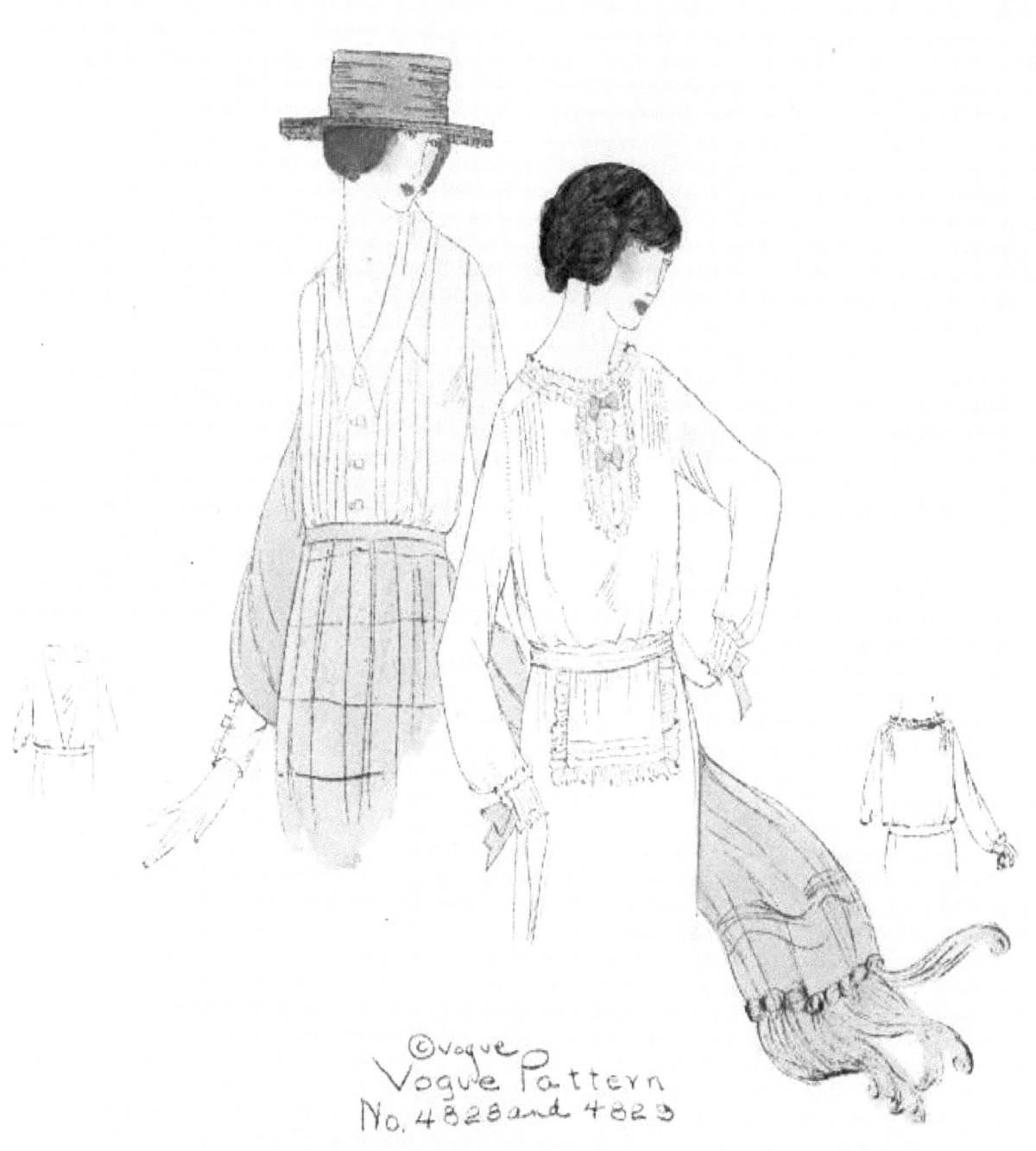

Vogue Pattern
No. 4828 and 4829

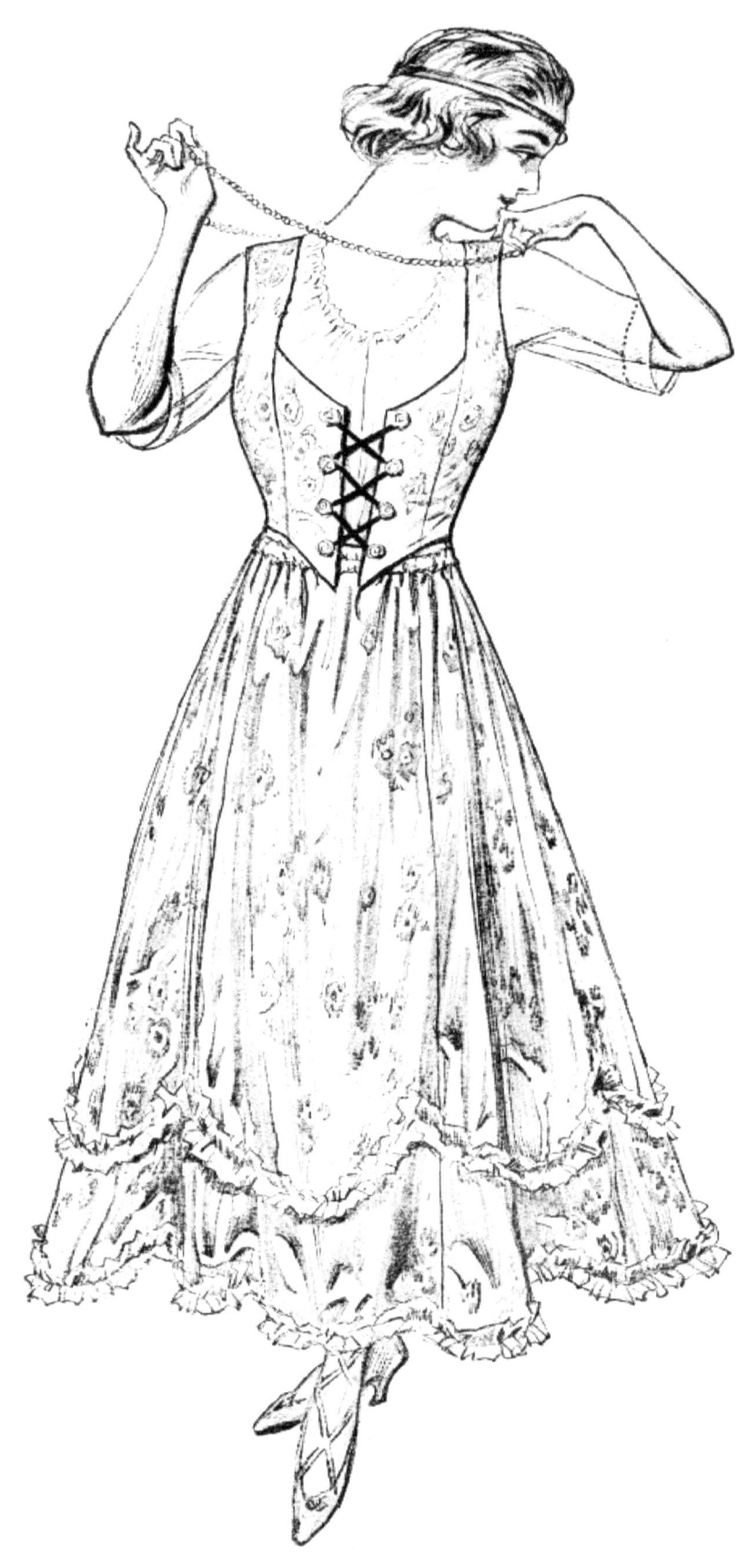

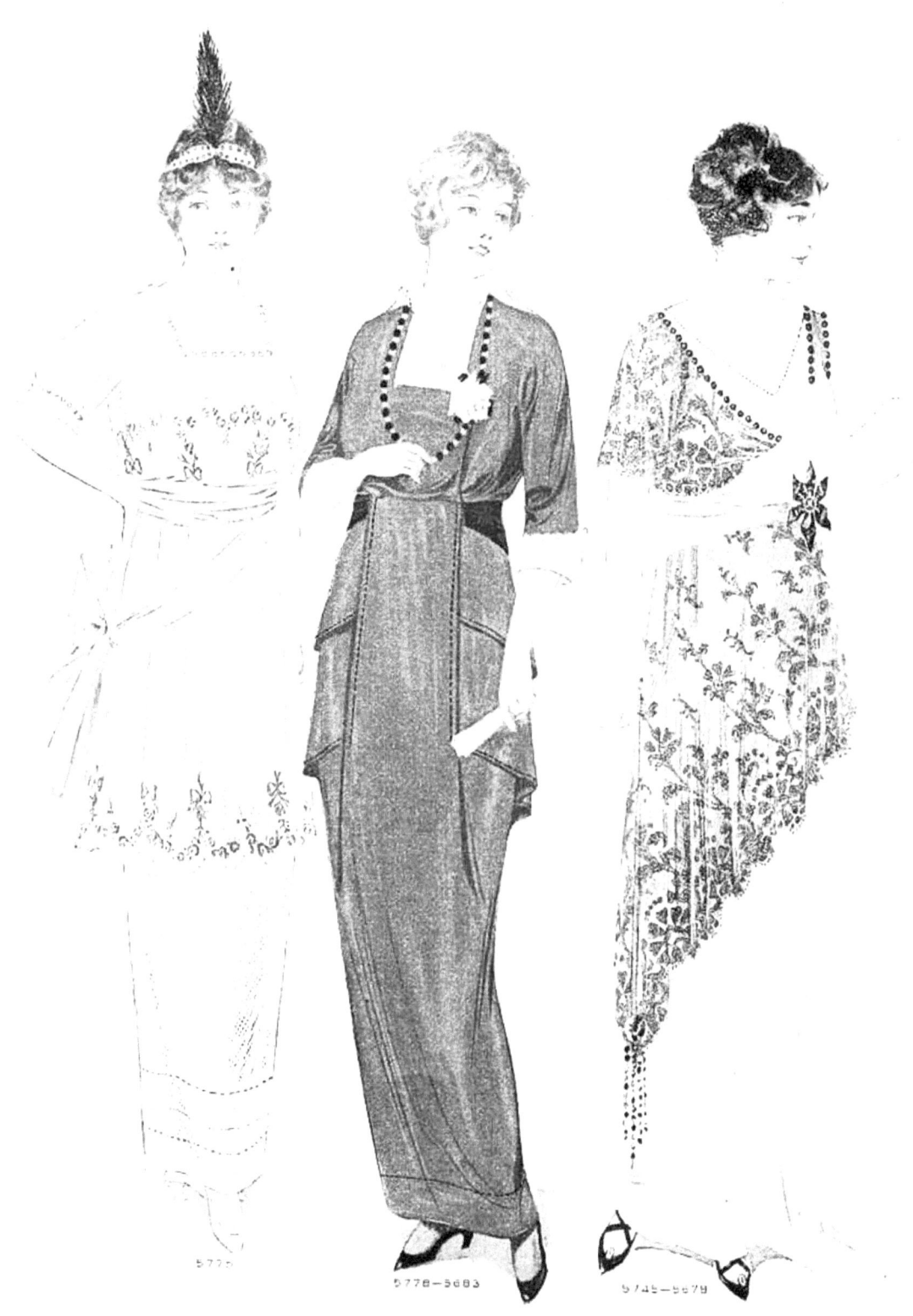

DAYTIME AND EVENING GOWNS OF DAINTY GRACE

THE VERY SIMPLICITY OF THESE MODELS MAKES THEM EFFECTIVE

For other views and decorations see page 45

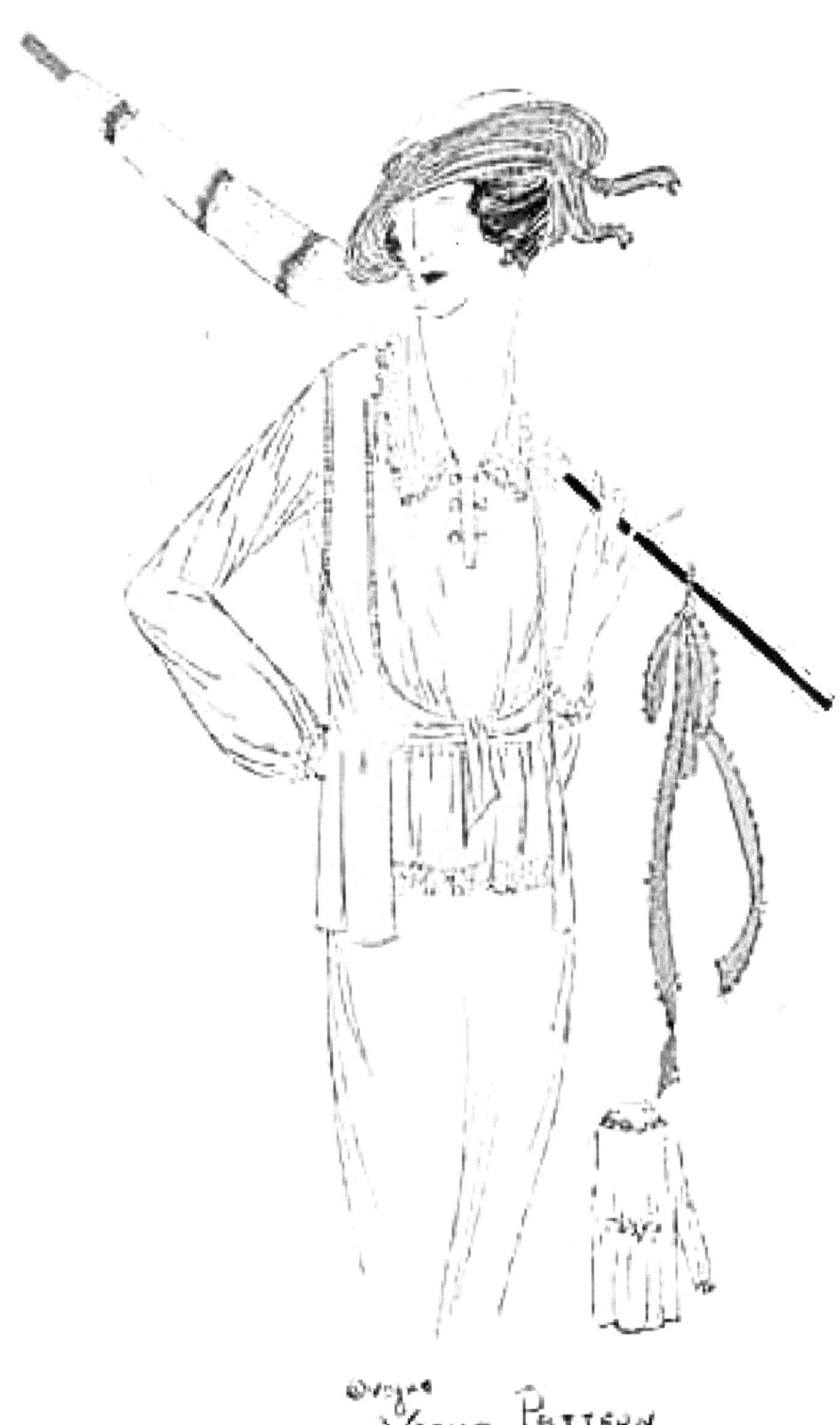

Vogue
Vogue Pattern
No. 4500

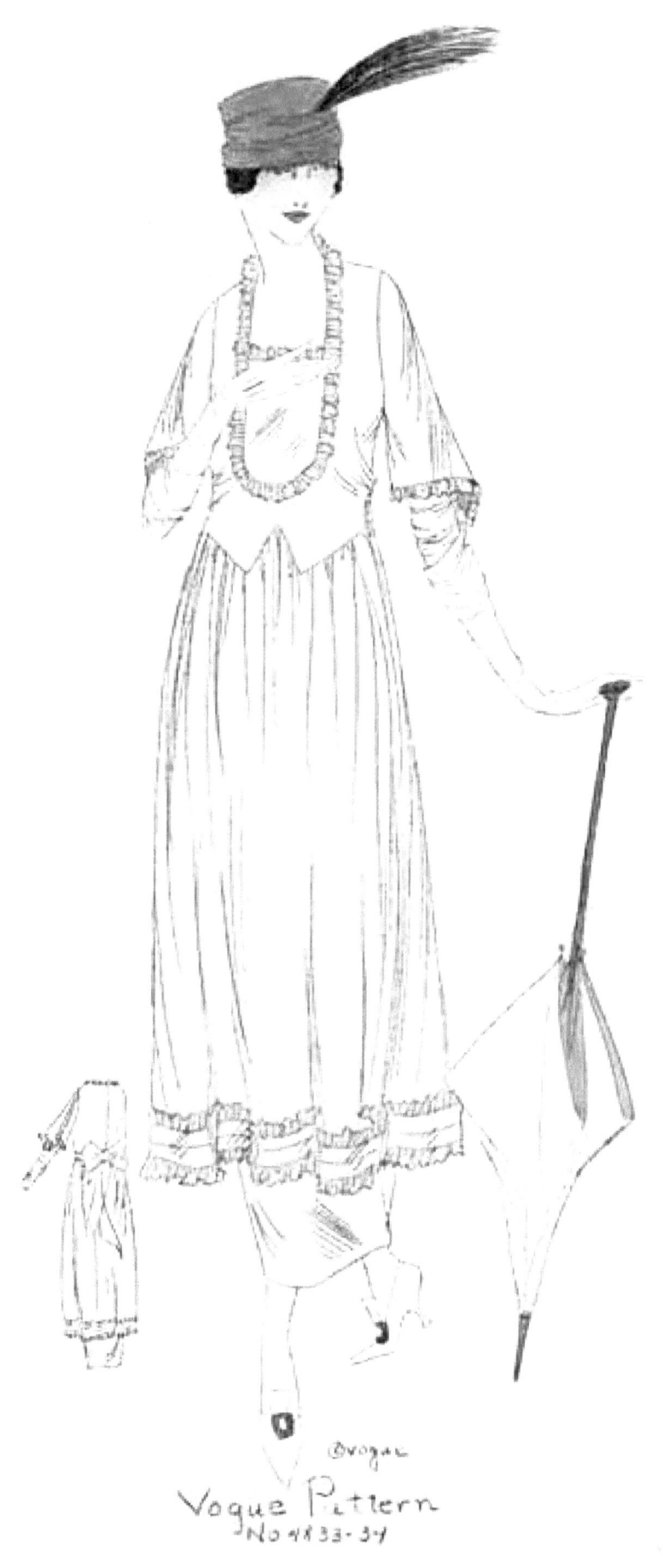

Vogue Pattern
No 4133-34

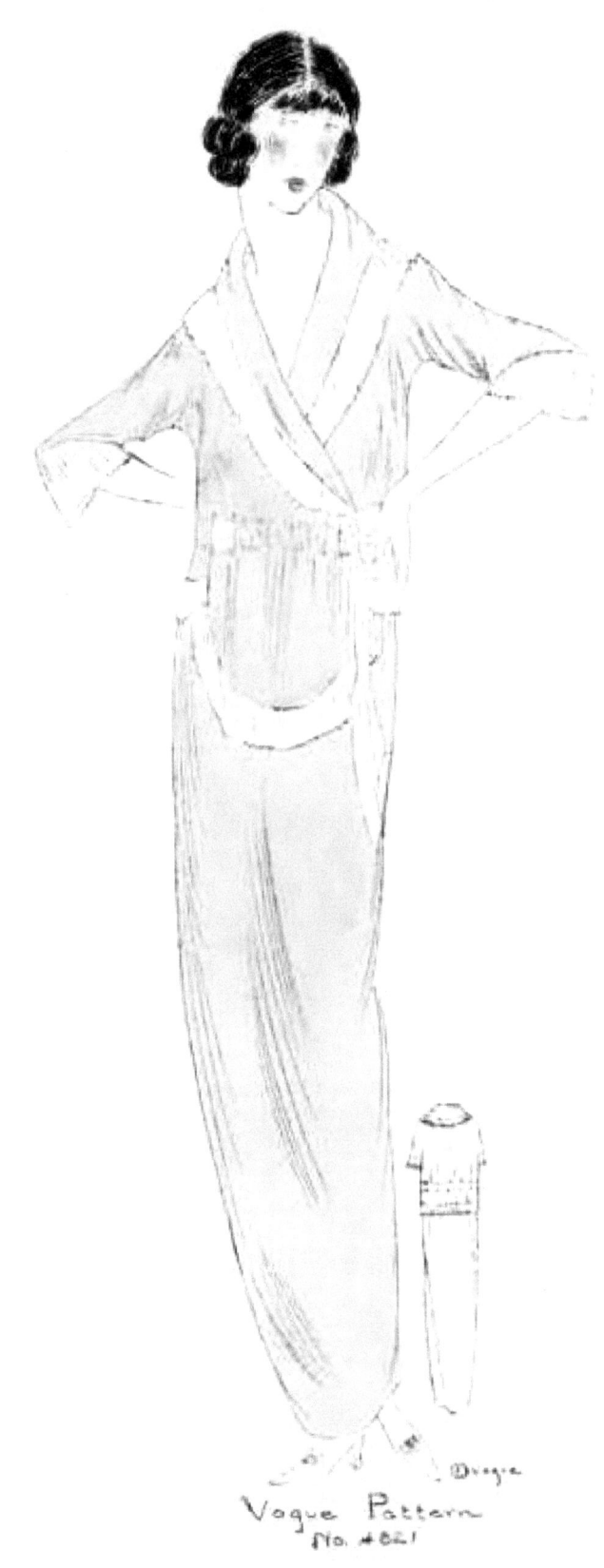

Vogue Pattern
No. #821

Pour le golf voici une robe de kasha
plissé dont le corsage est garni de
ganses de laine vertes et rouges.
Un kasha quadrillé de façon originale
fait cette robe ceinturée de moire et
cravatée de faille rouge.

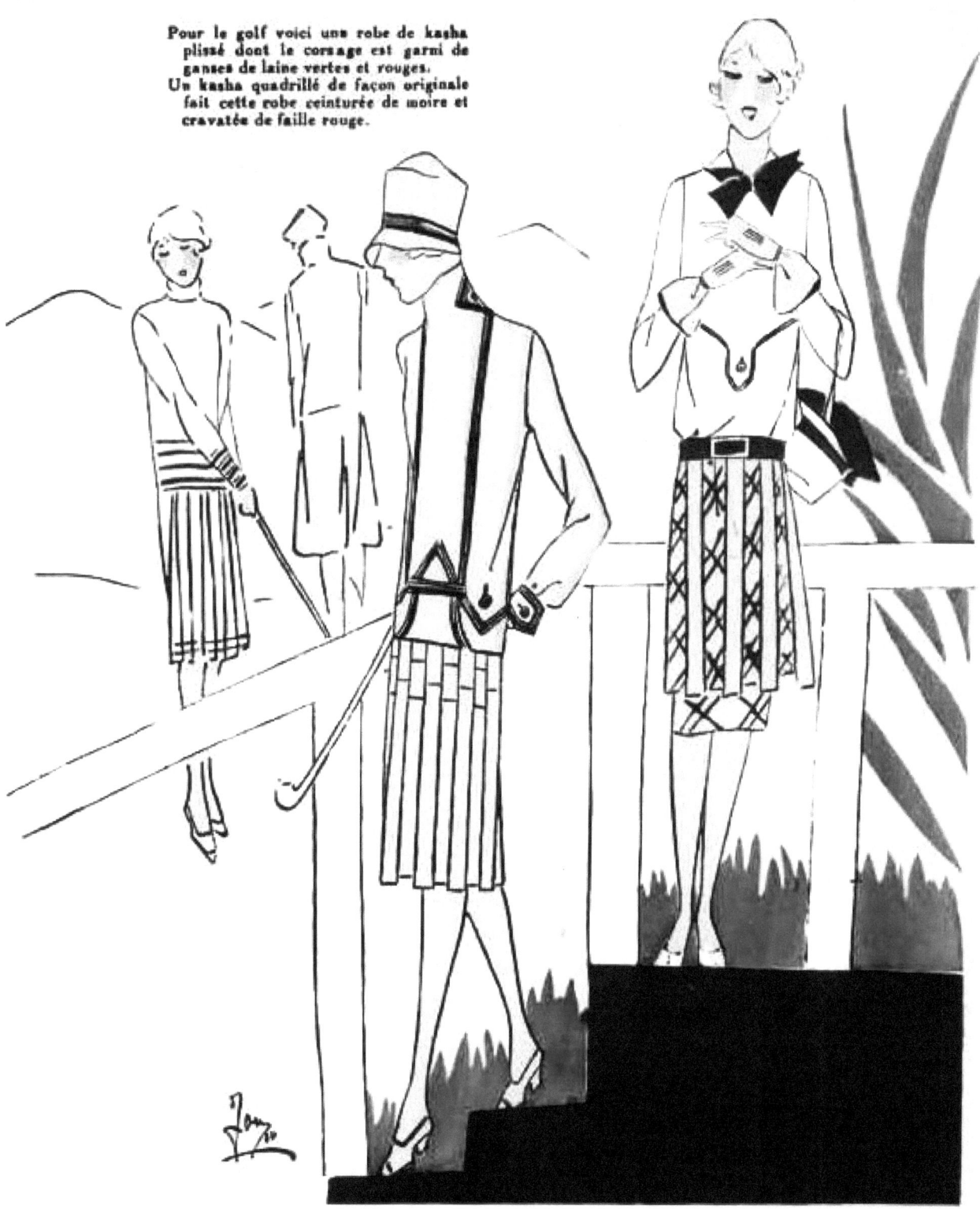

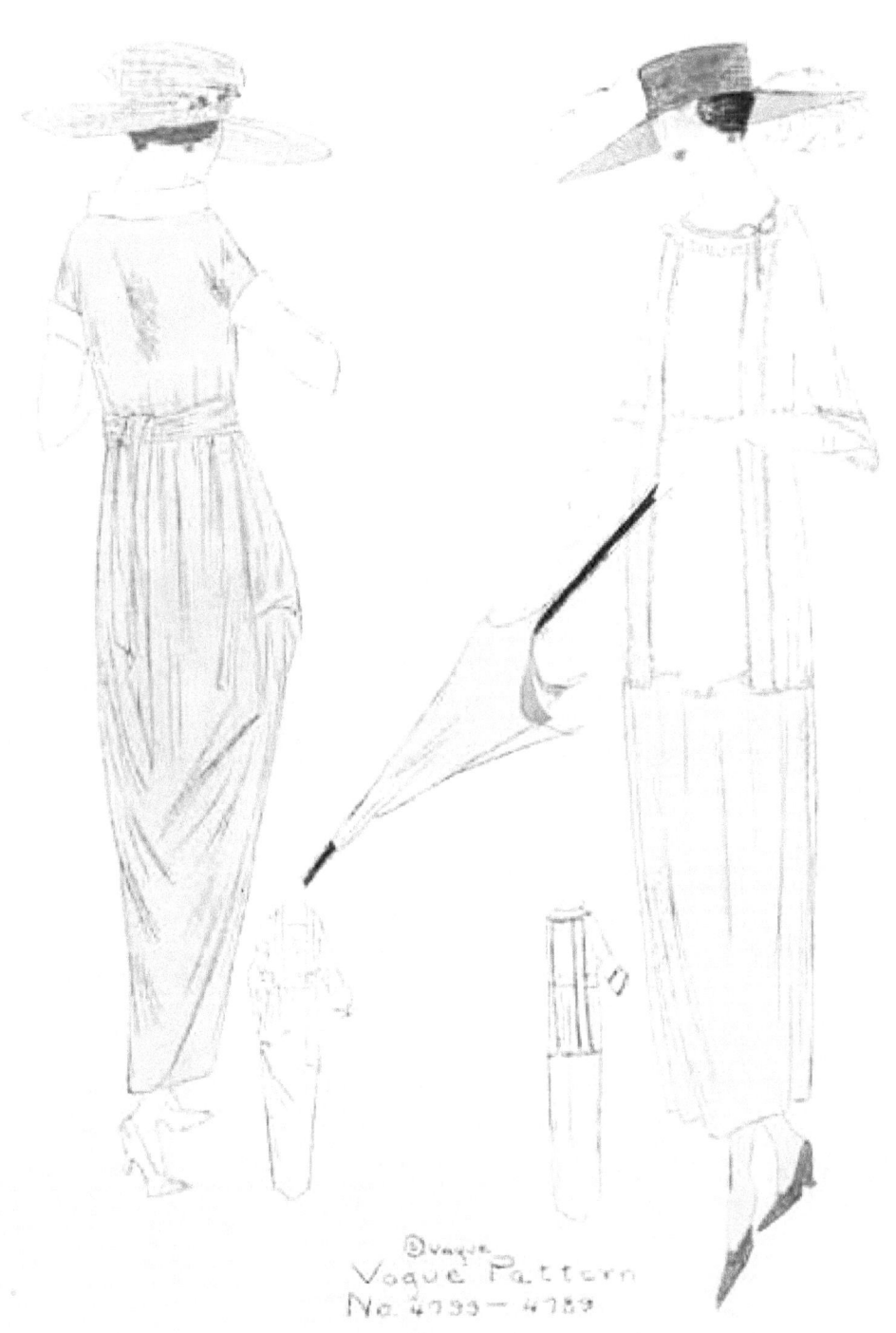

Vogue Pattern
No. 4799 — 4789

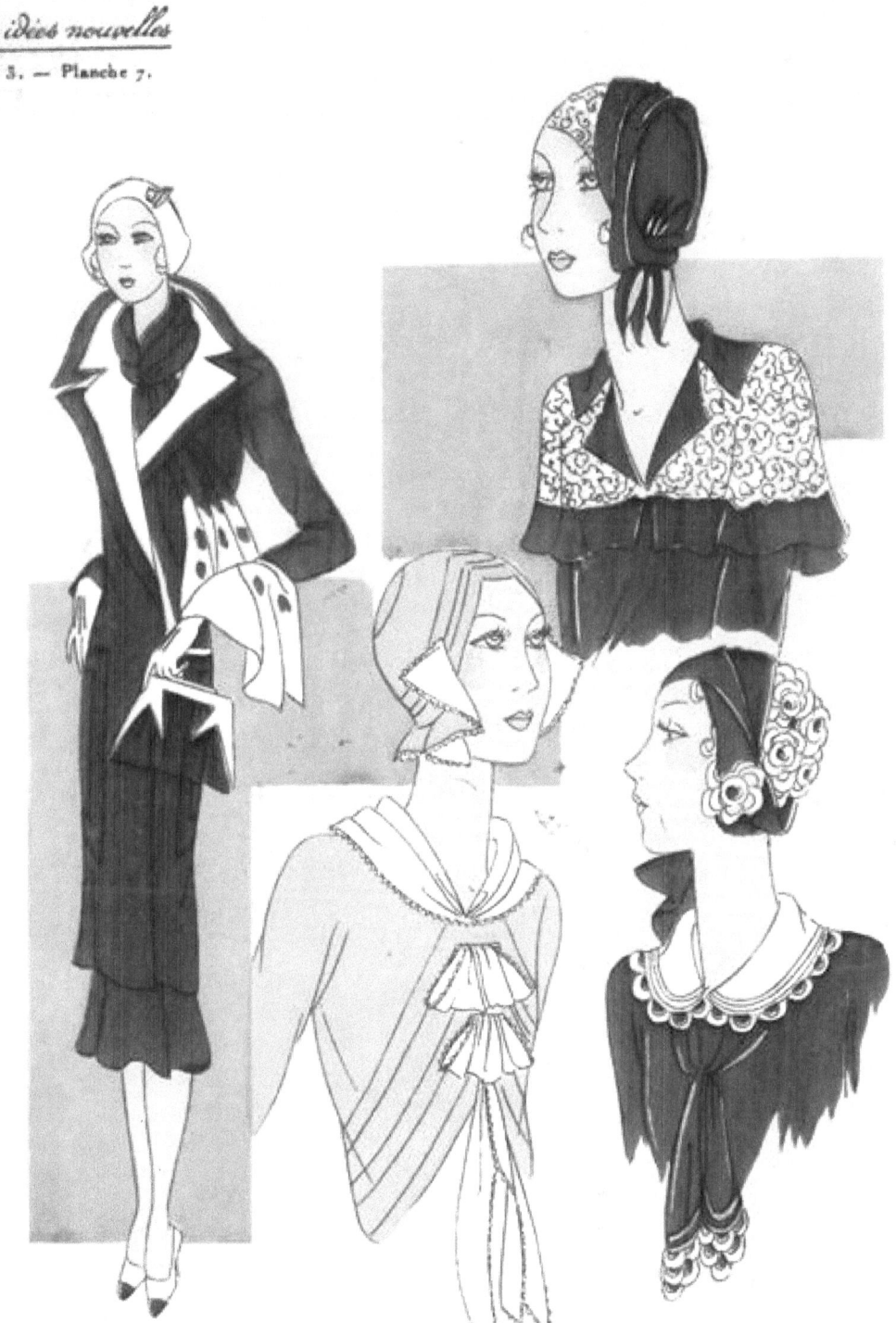

Ensemble en marocain bleu toile garni de piqué blanc. Le chapeau, l'écharpe et le sac sont assortis. — Berthe de dentelle brodée, plongeante dans le dos et soulignée d'un biais de georgette. Le béret plat de côté est assorti et garni de trois plumes laquées. — Robe et bonnet de romain bleu pastel éclaircis de même tissu blanc bordé de fines dents. — Robe et bonnet de satin marine agrémentés de coquilles de satin blanc.

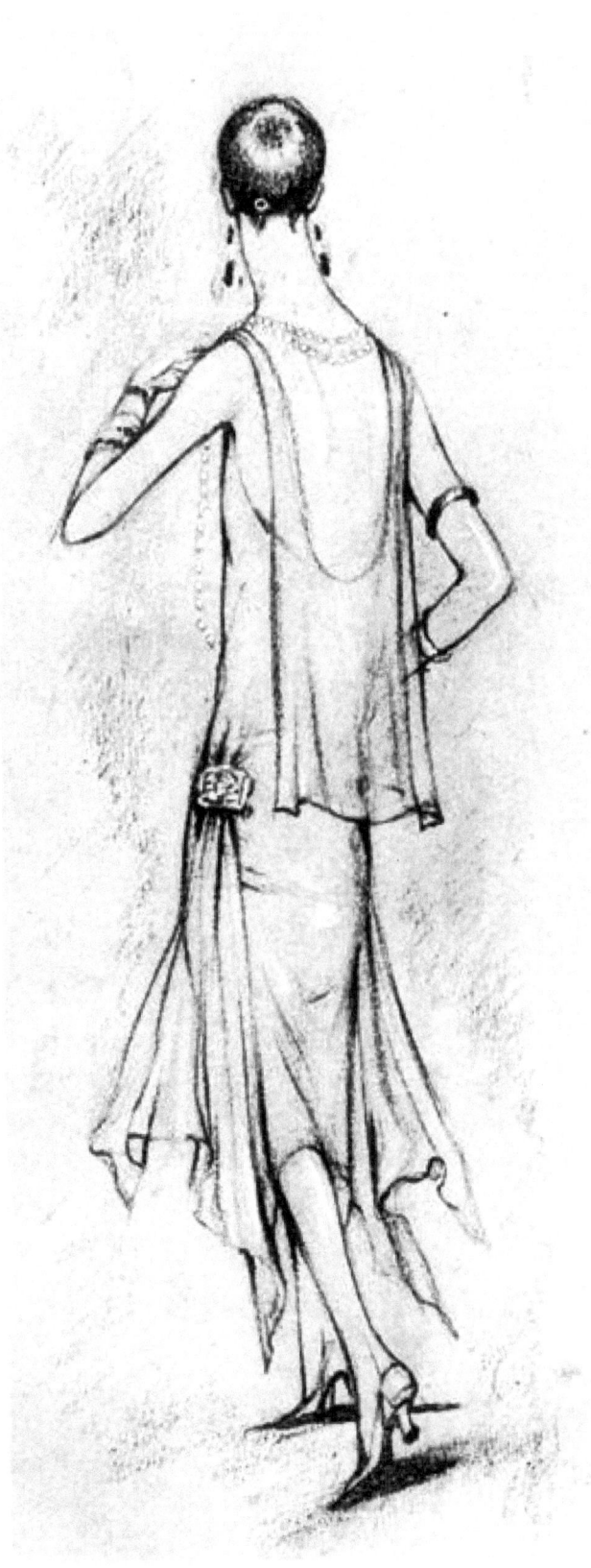

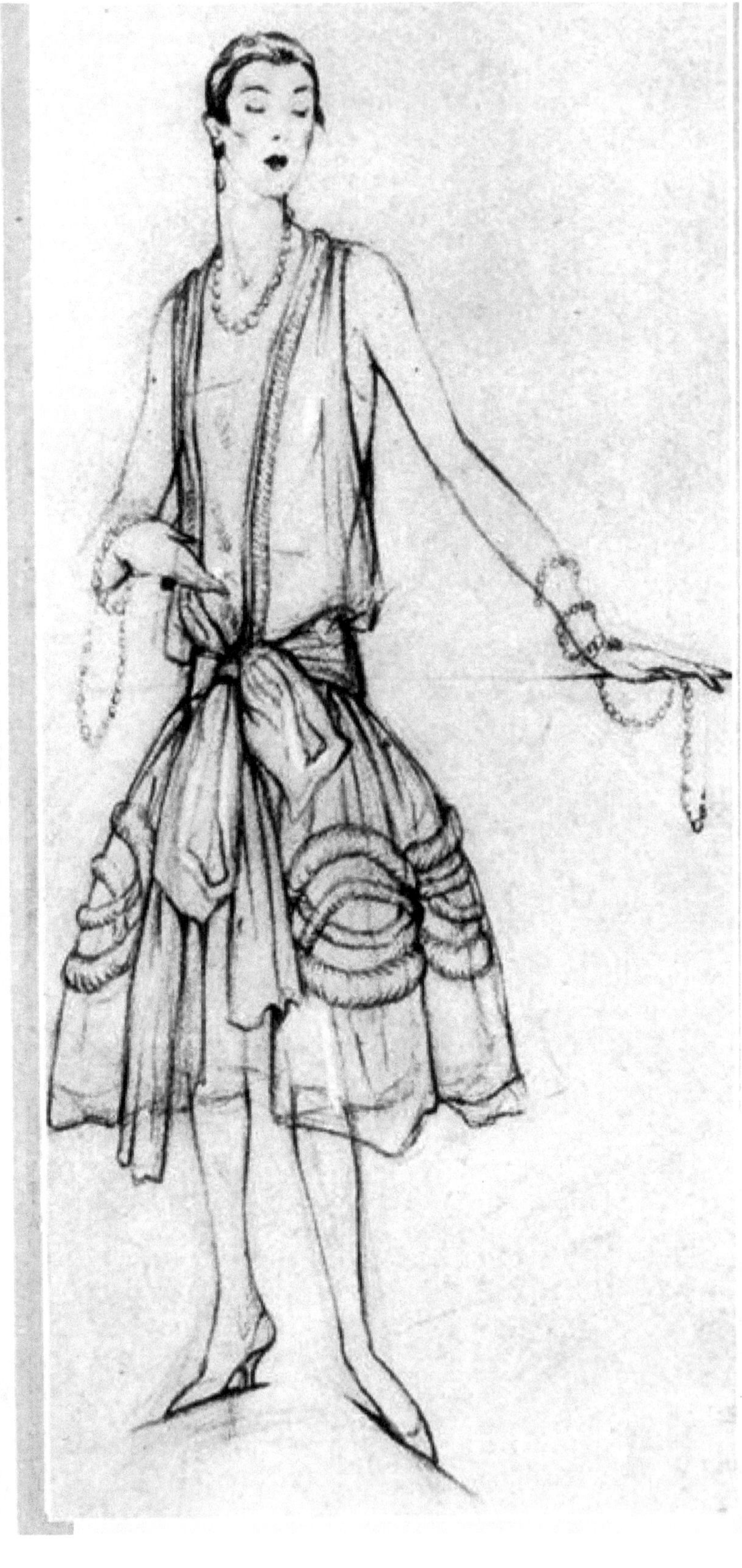

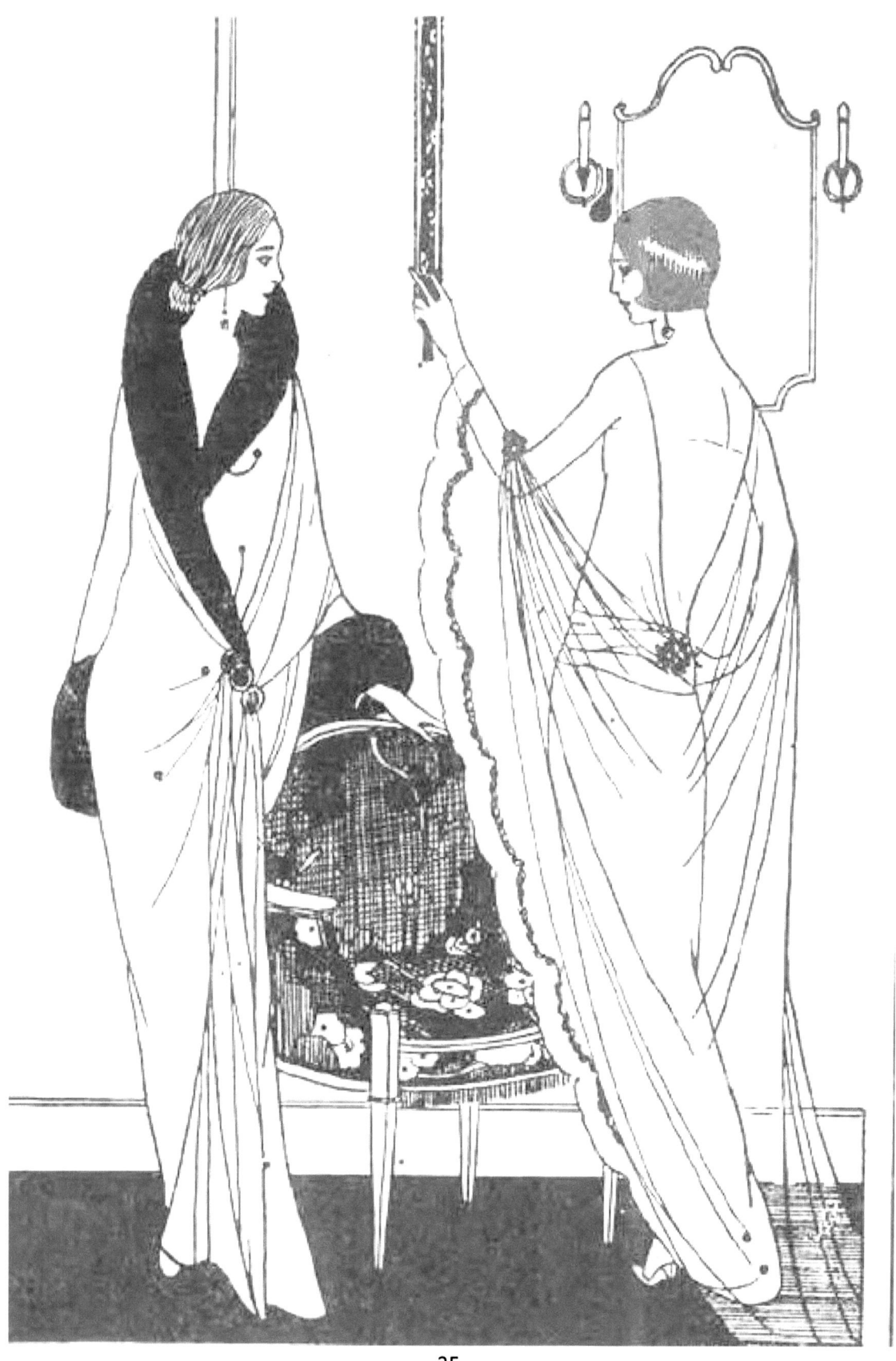

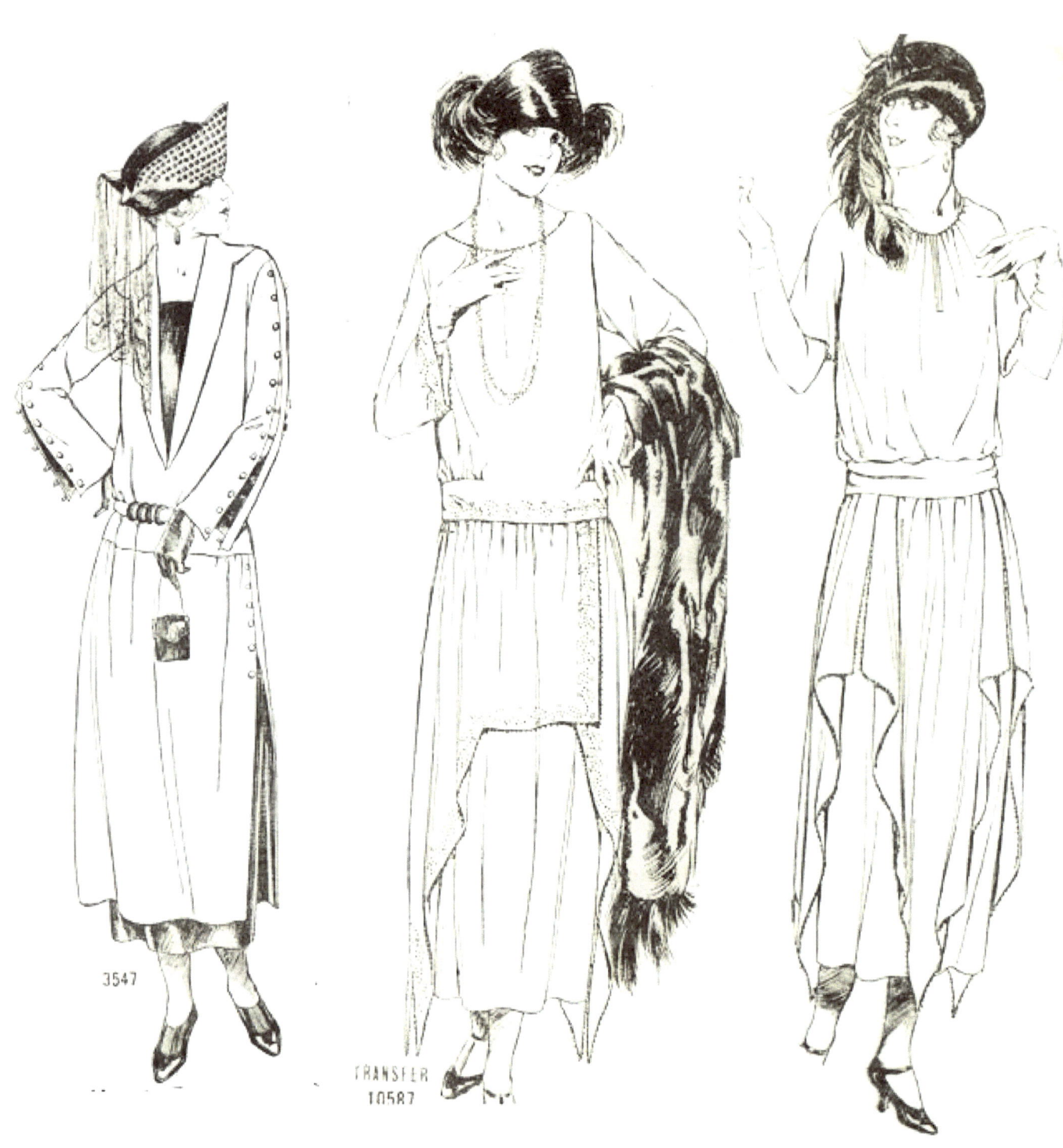

3547

TRANSFER
10587

26

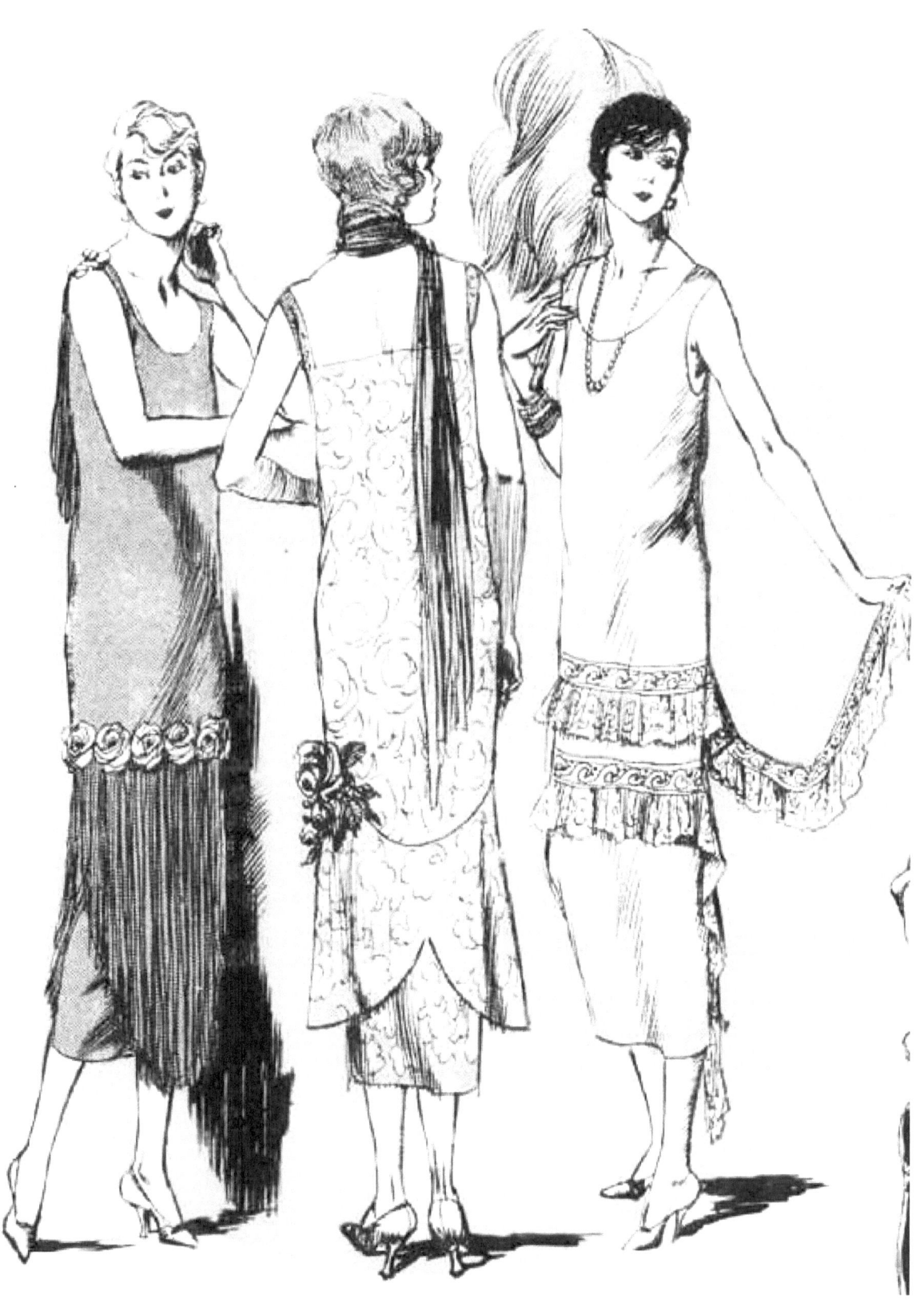

By the Sea, By the Beautiful Sea

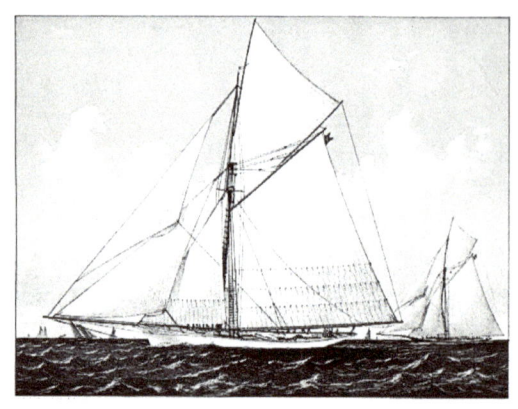

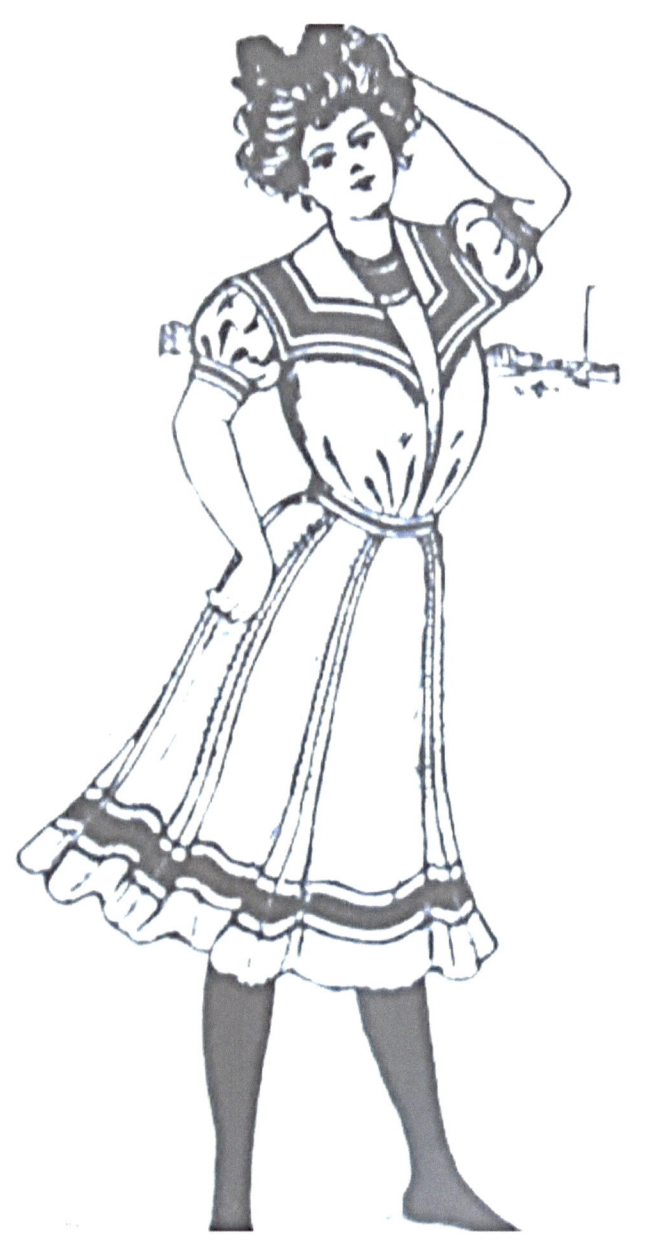

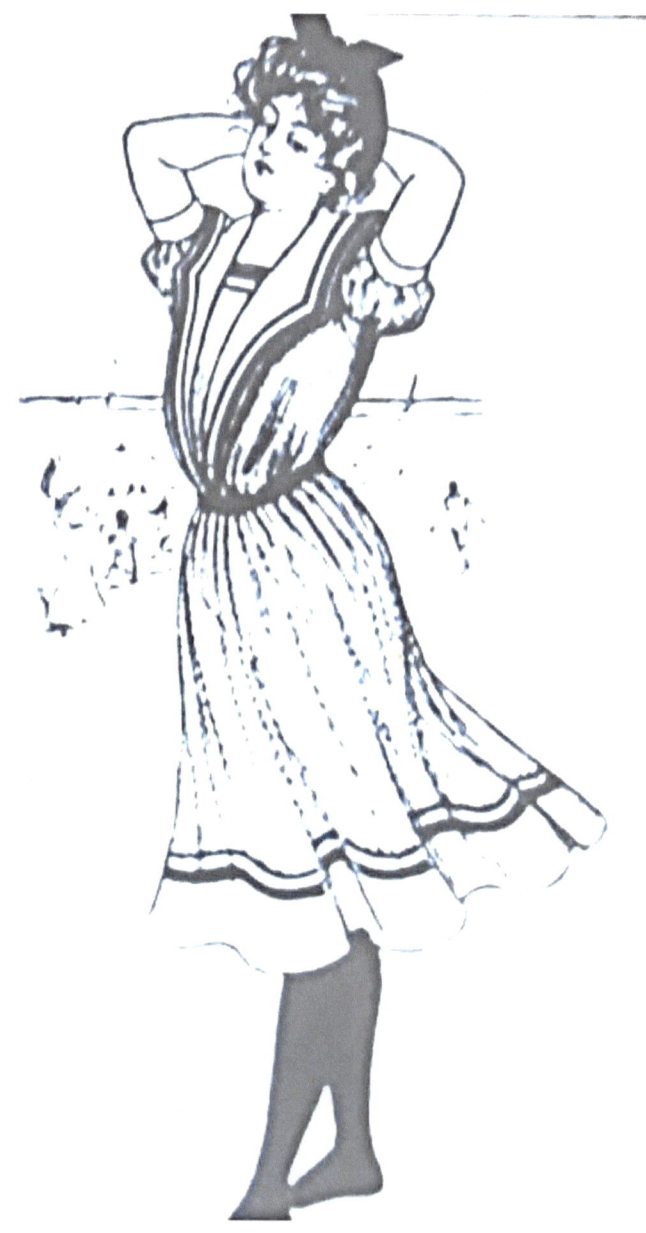

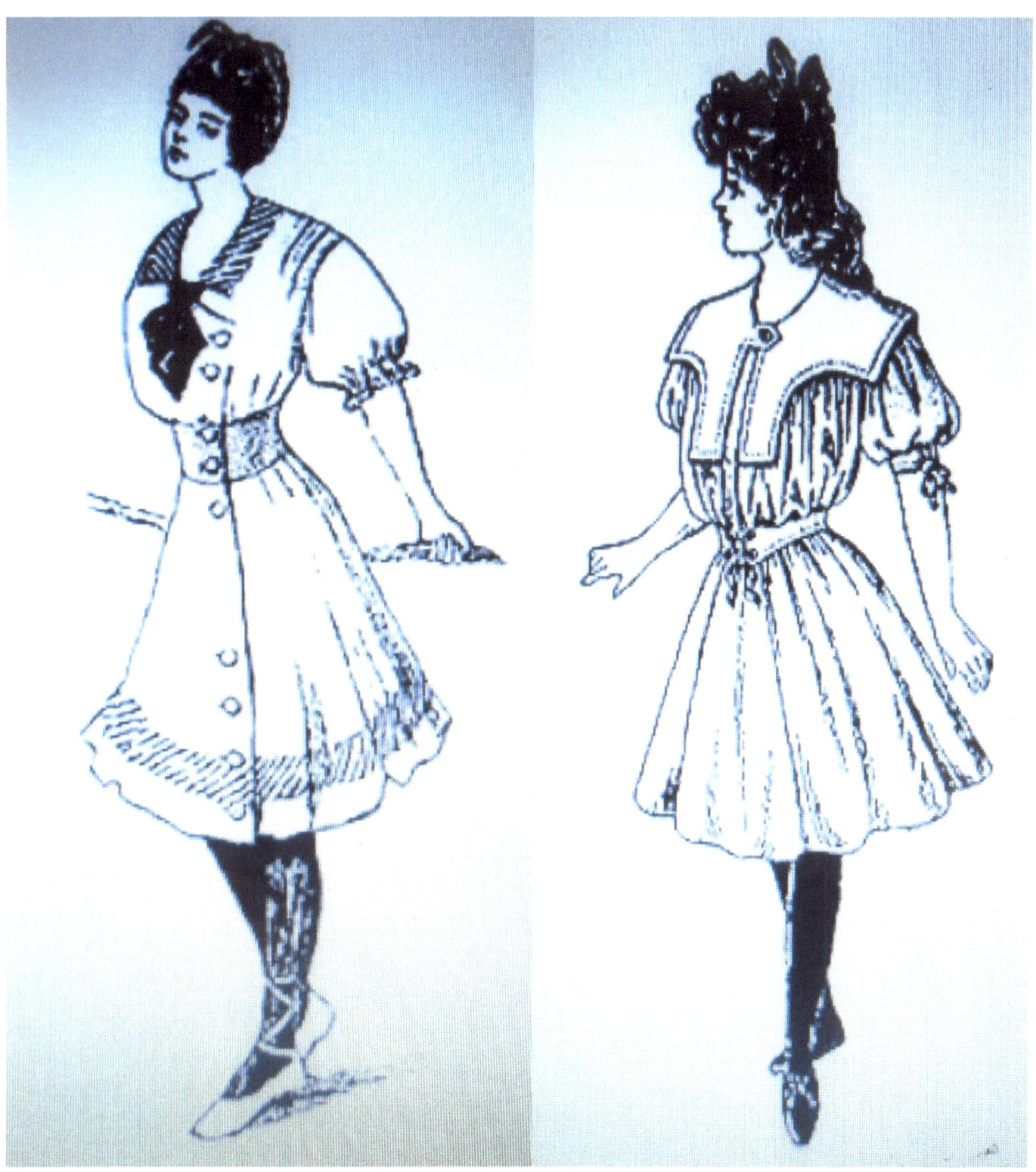

29

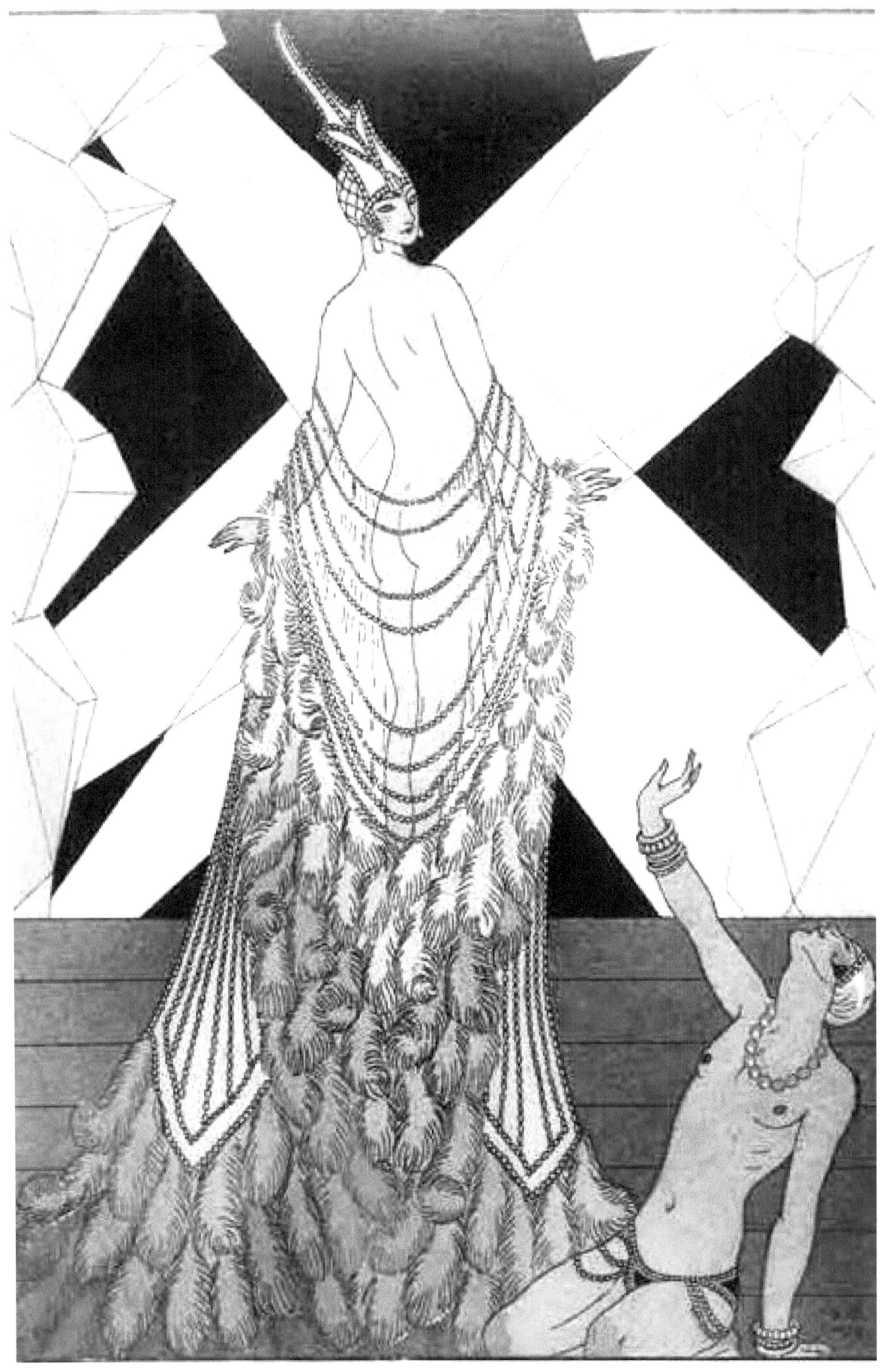

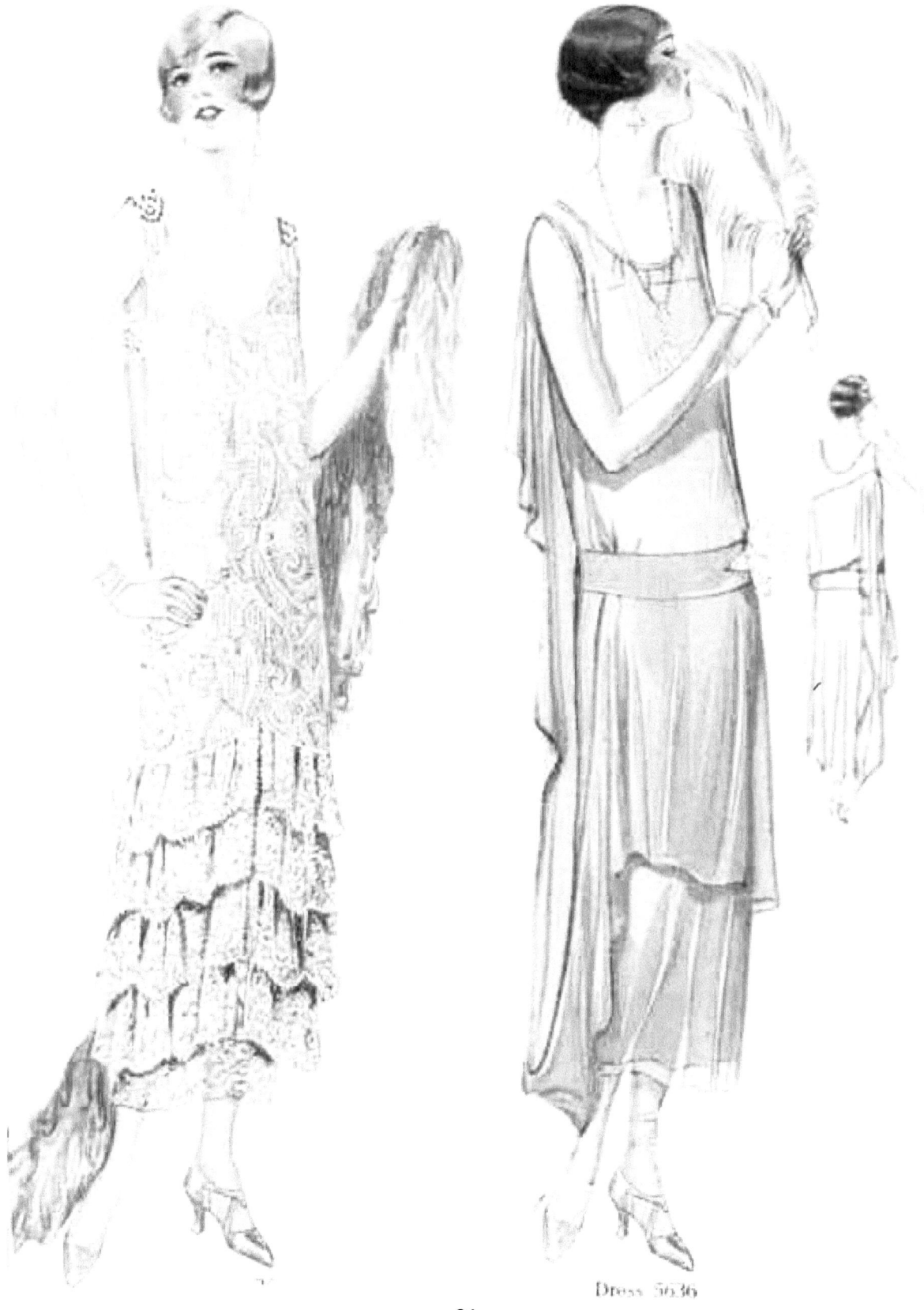

1924

Dress 56.36

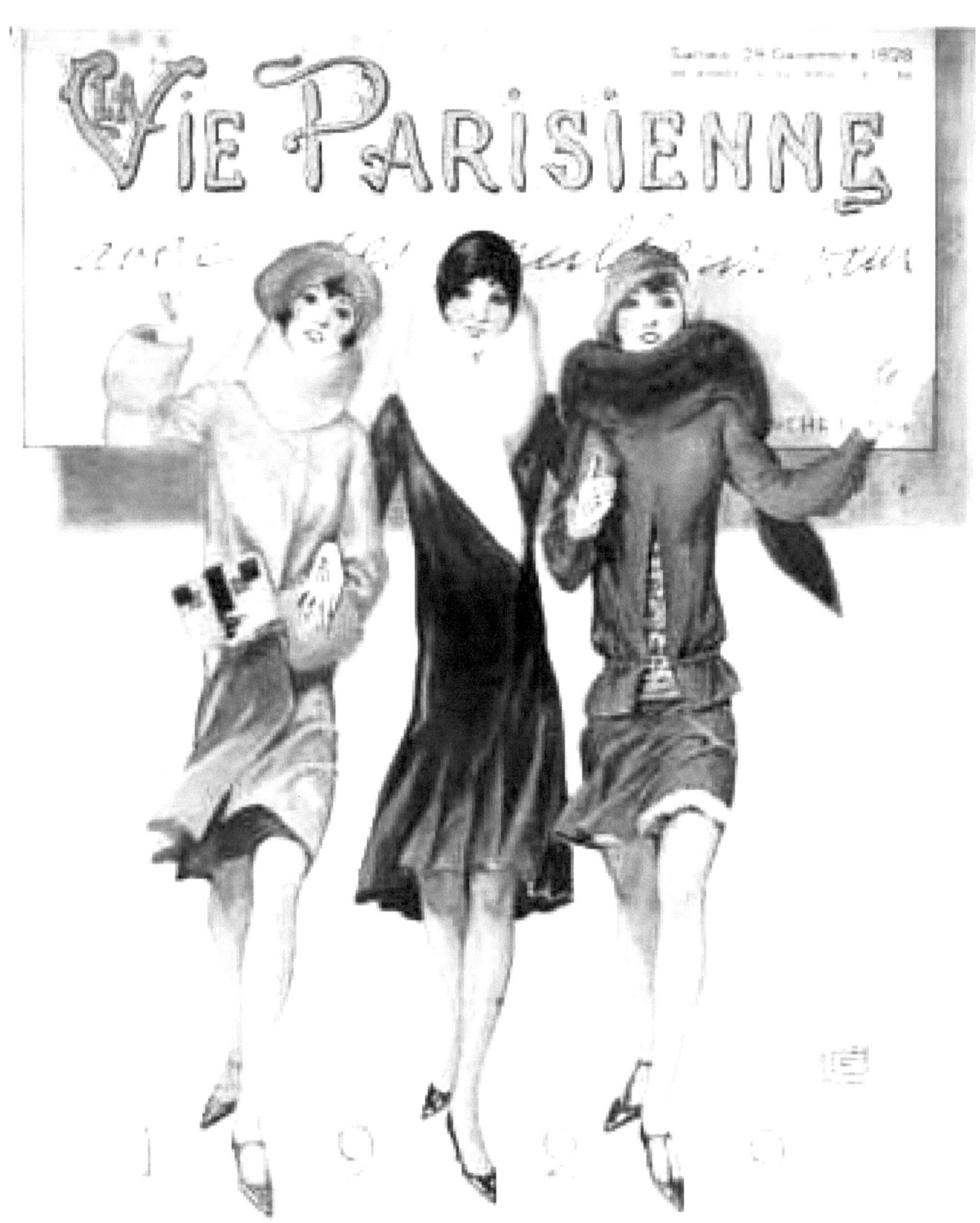

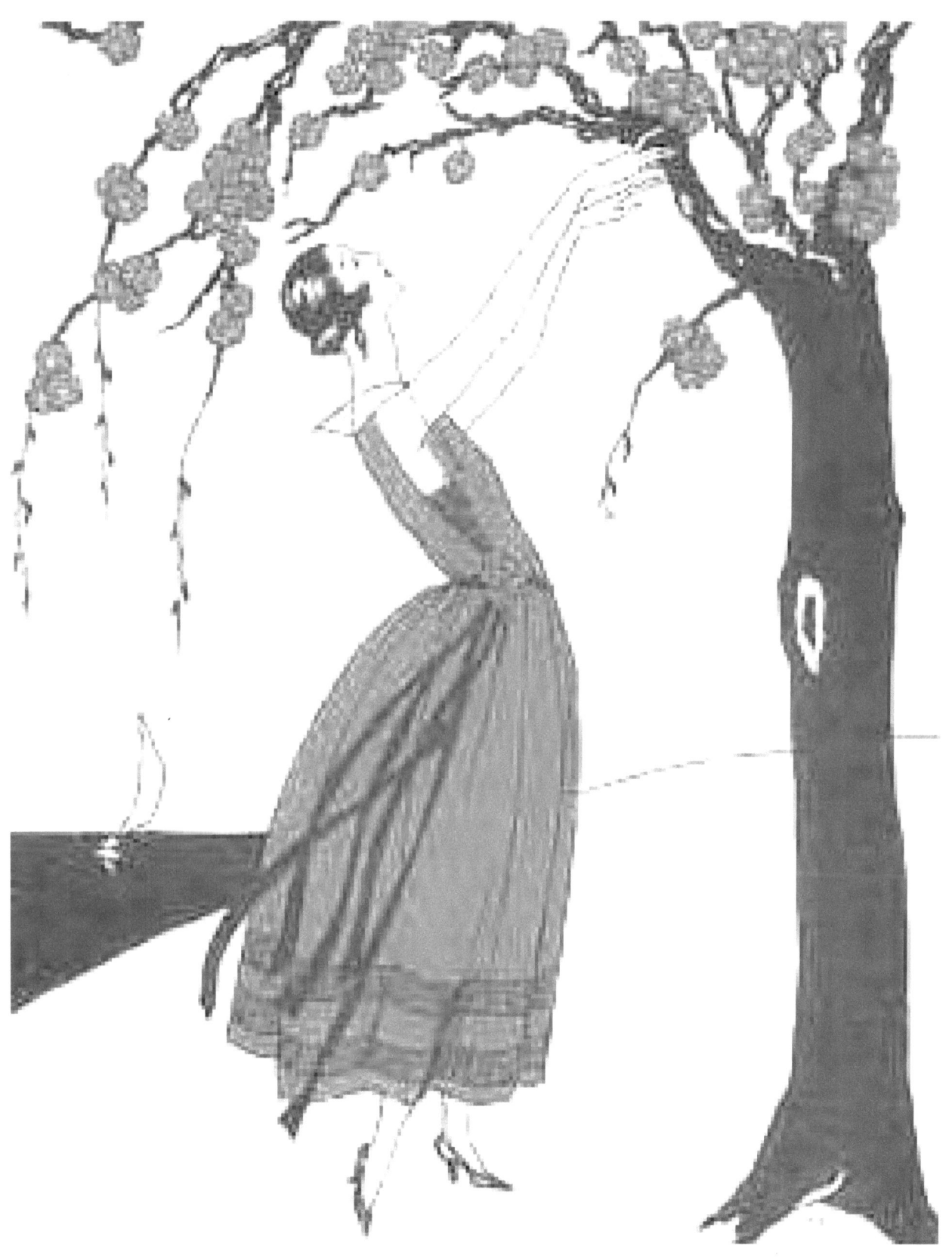

VOGUE

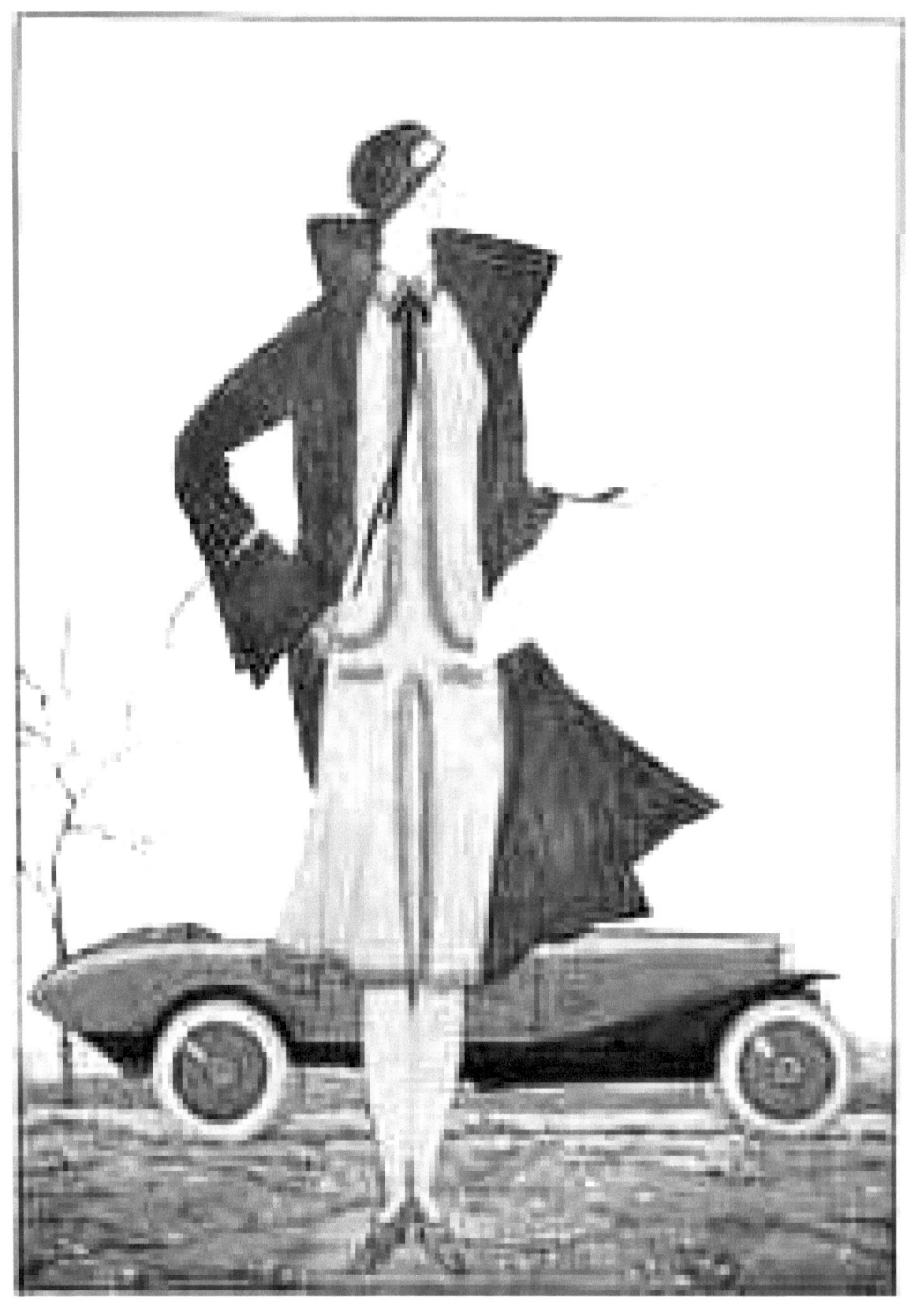

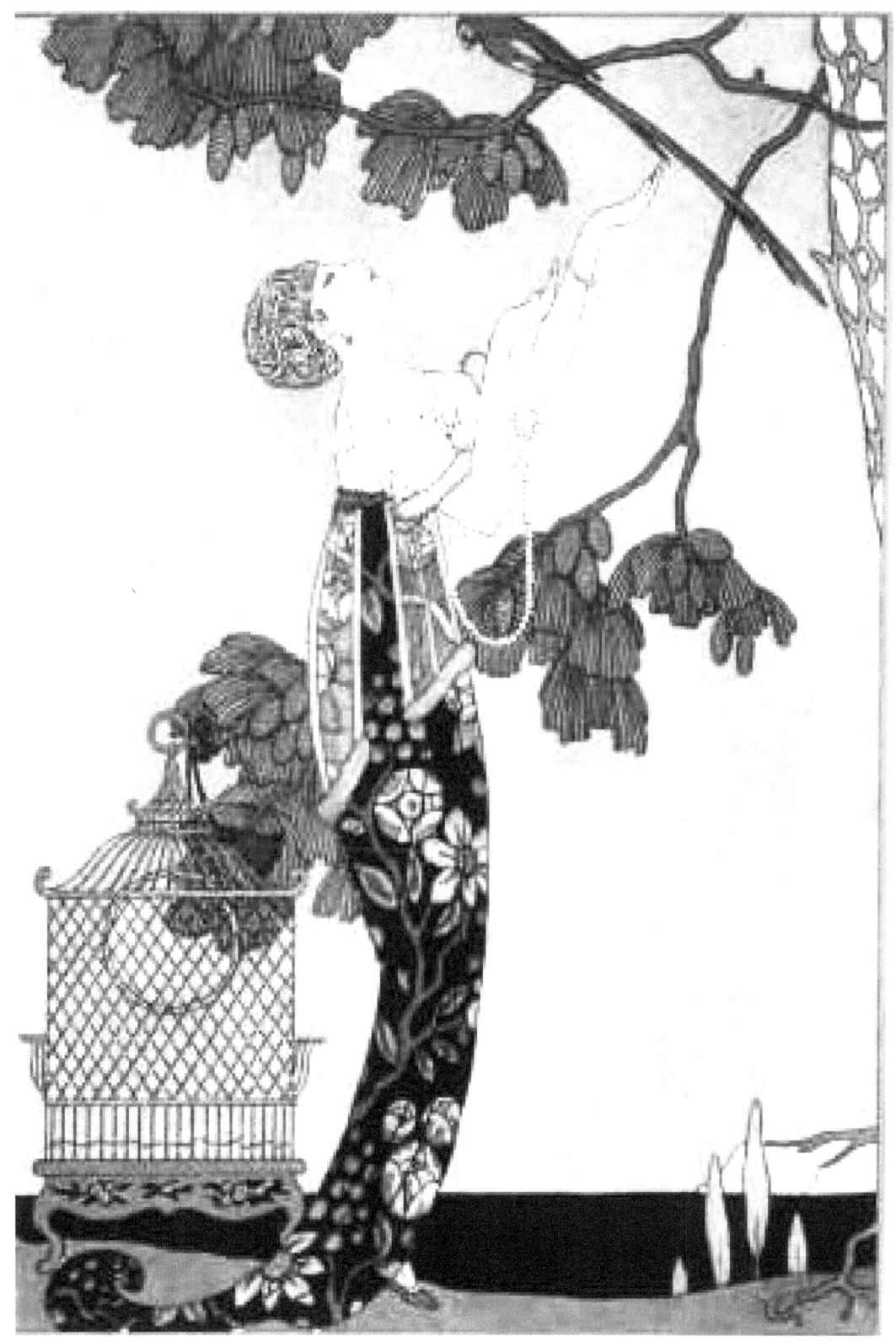

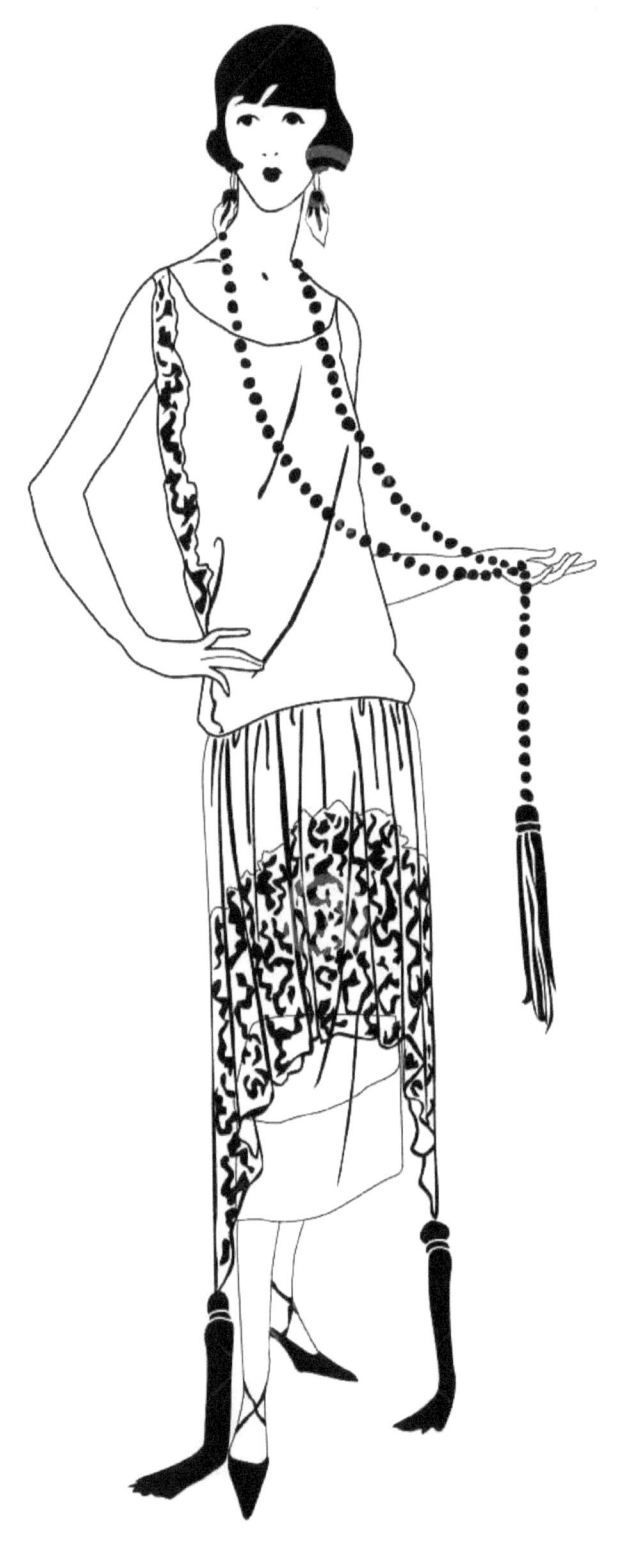

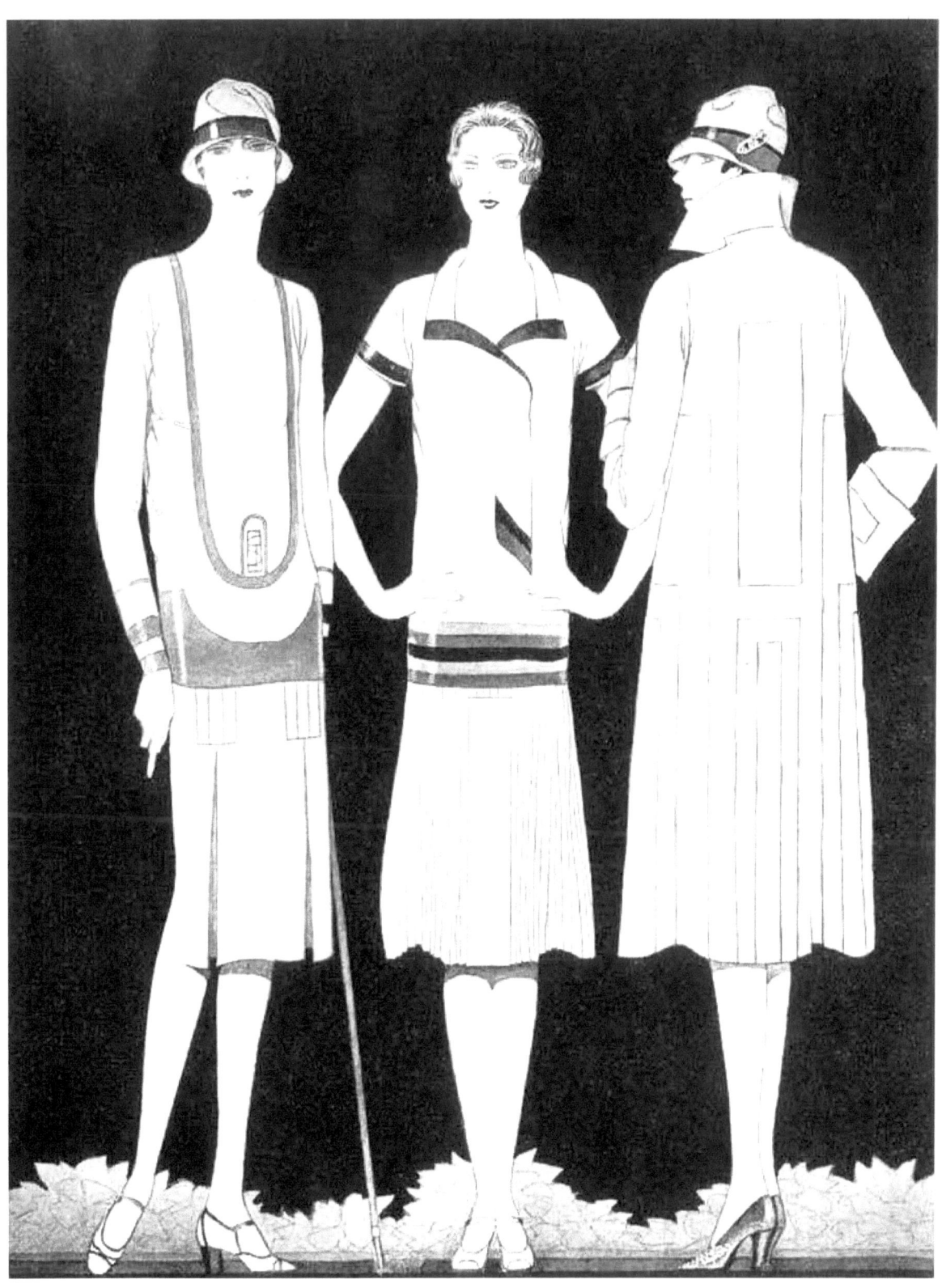

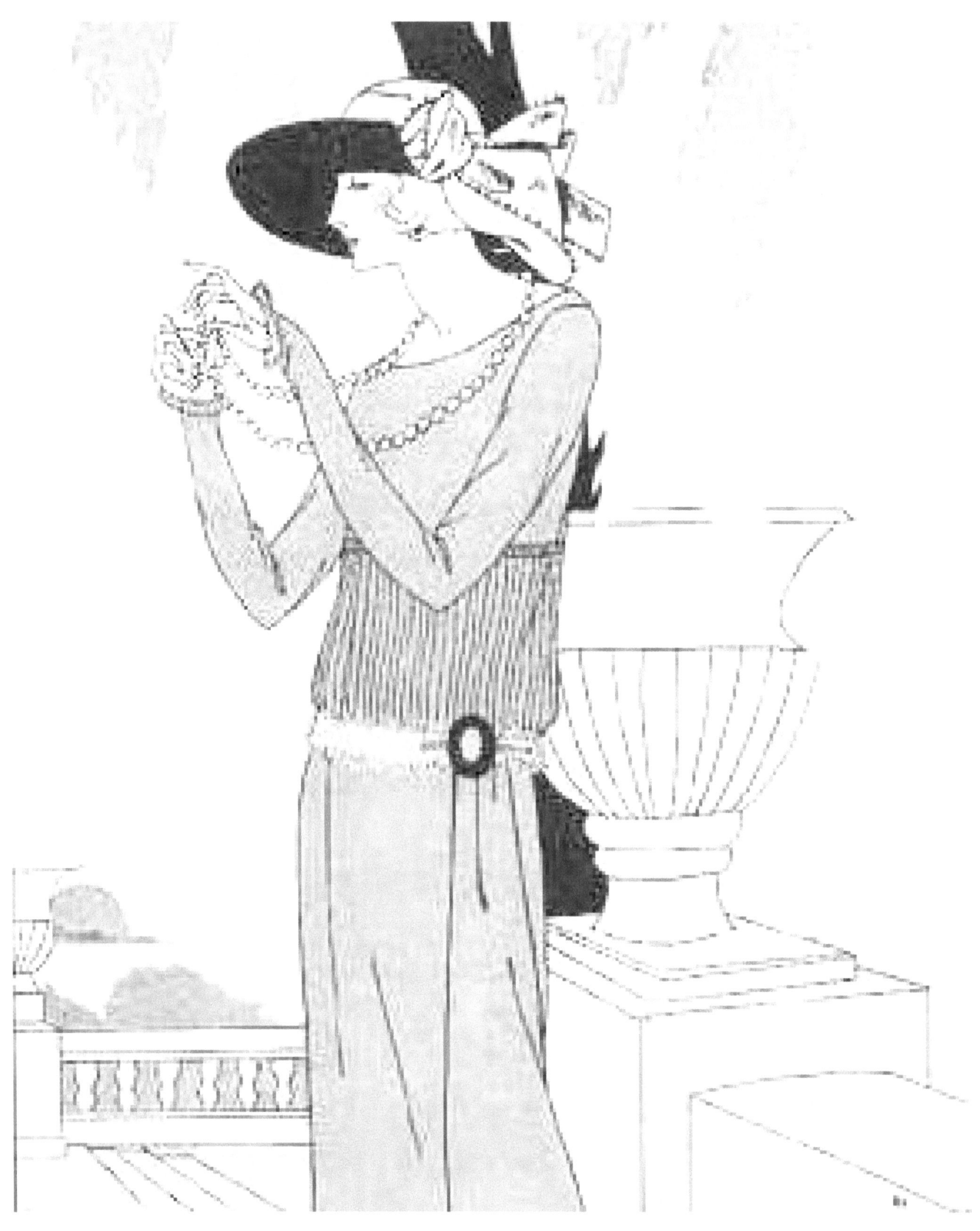

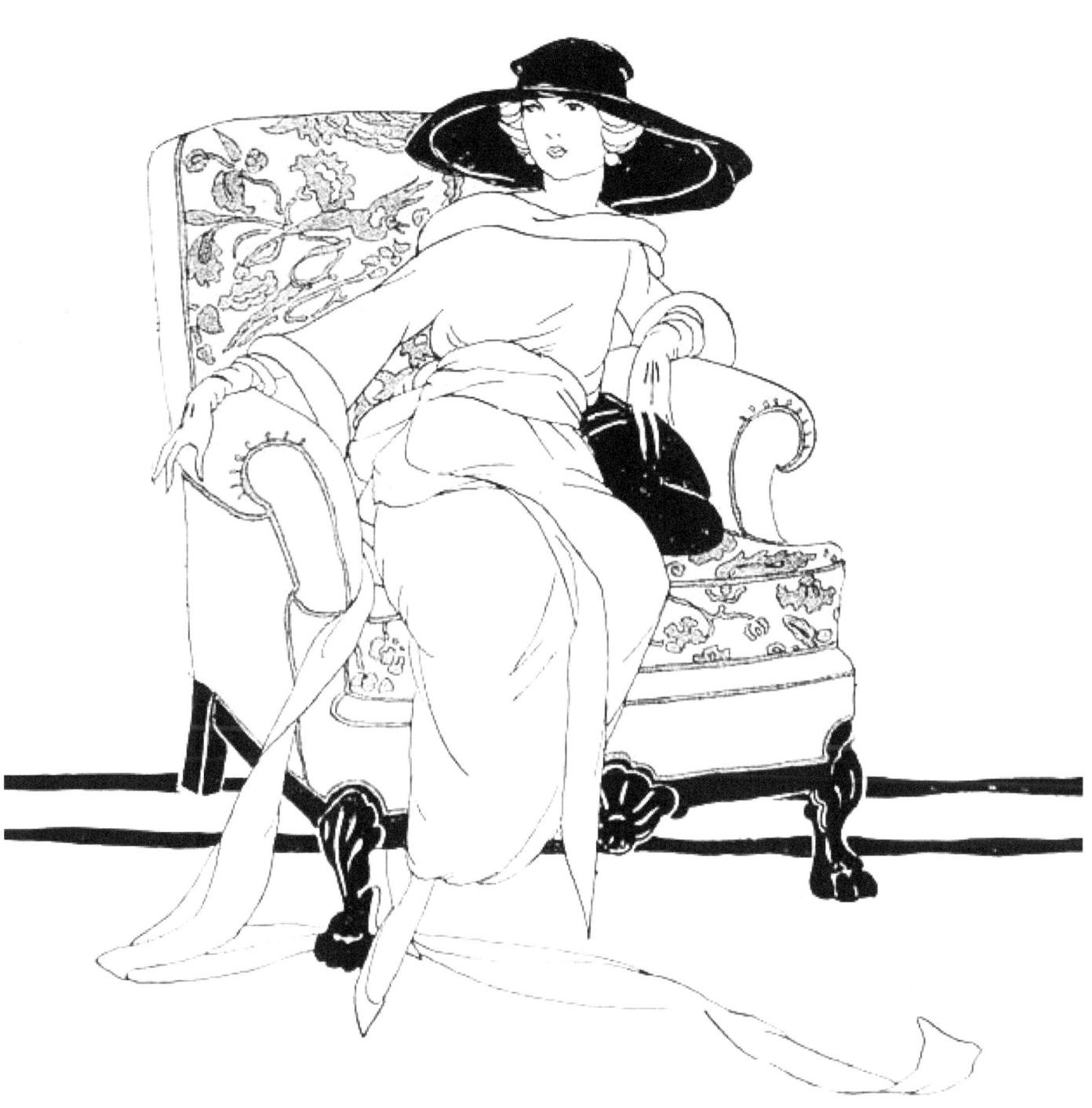

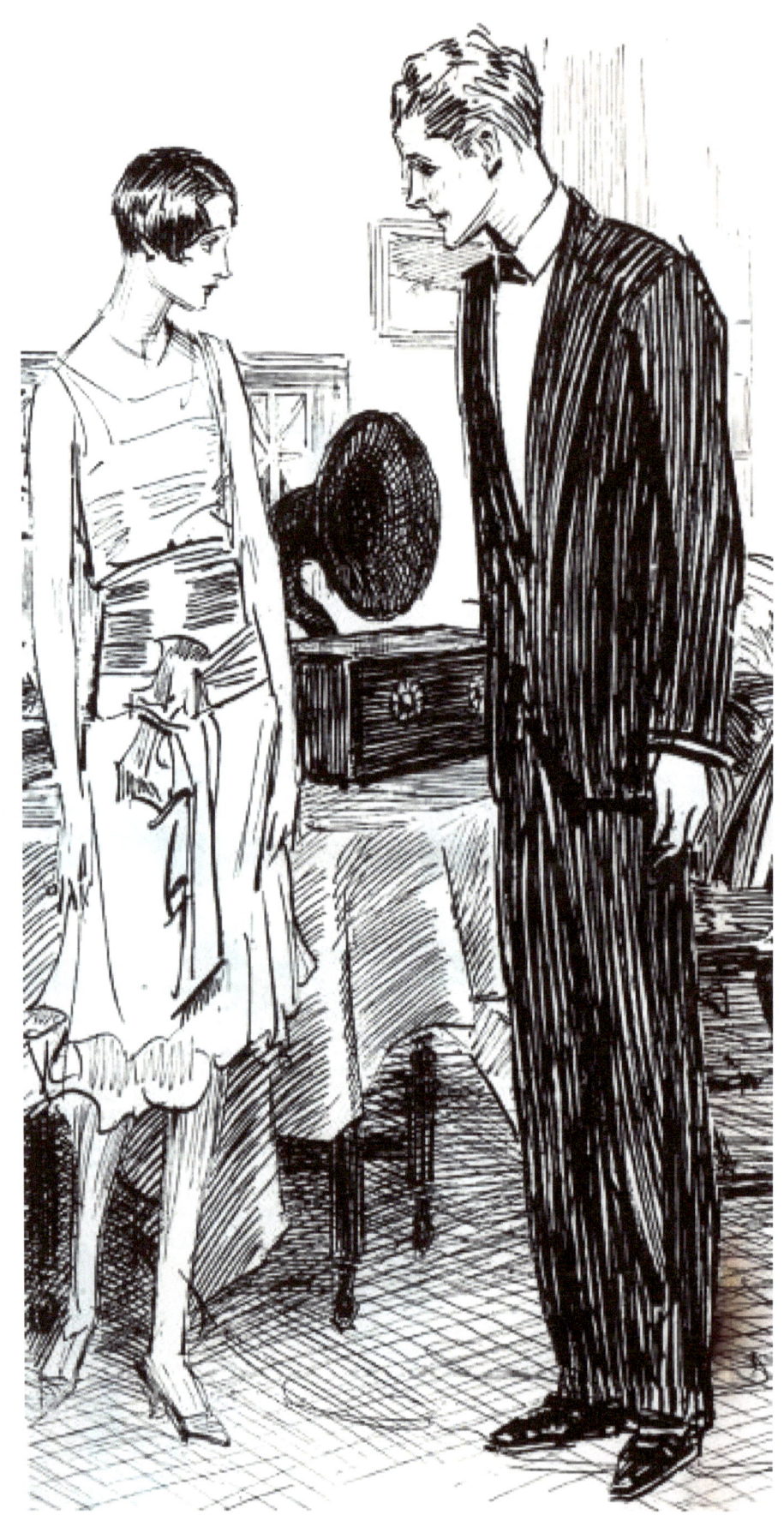

1920-1930 Hairstyles

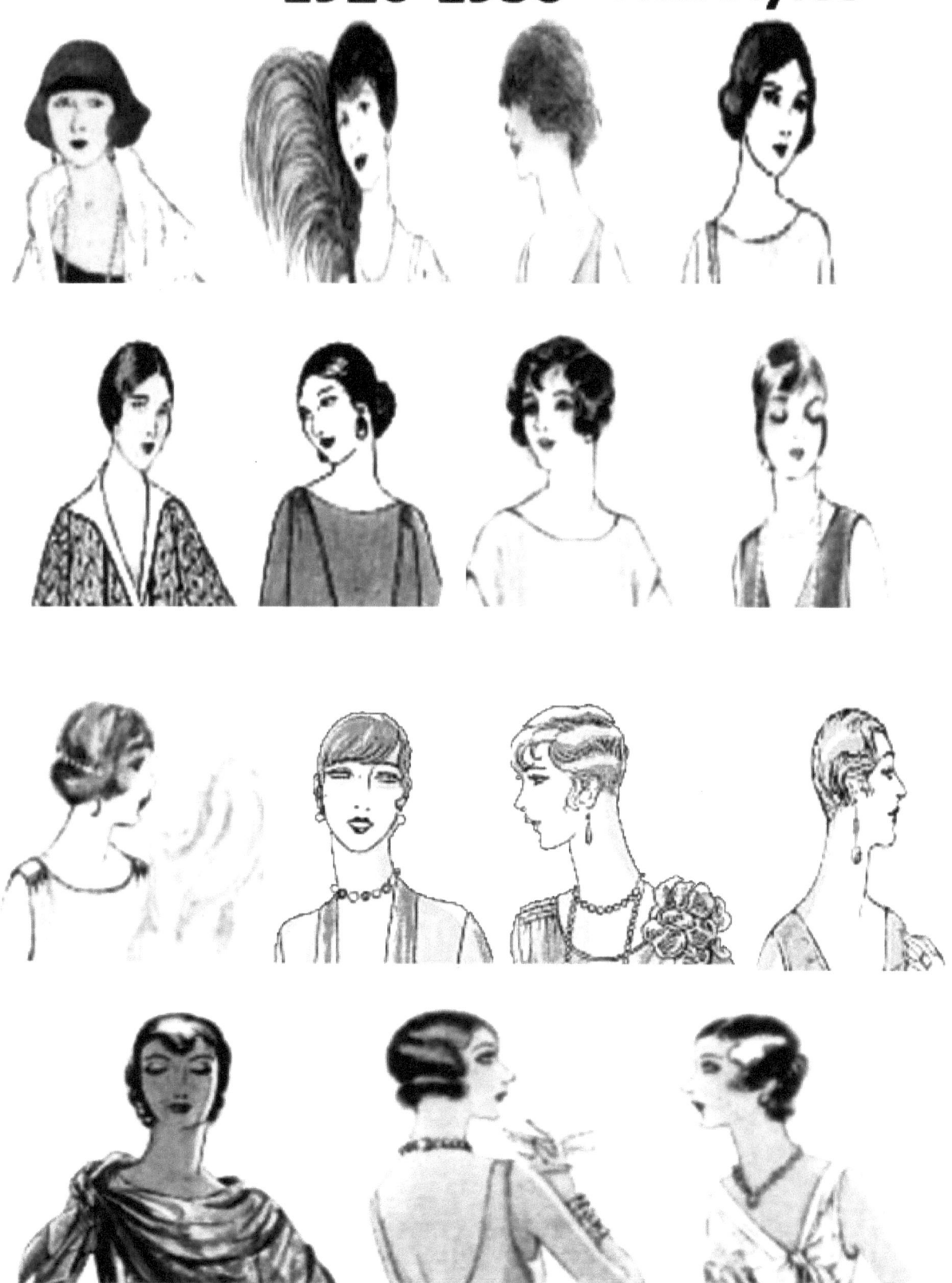